FEARFULLY AND WONDERFULLY MADE

THE FASTING BOOK

(A New Fresh Perspective of Yourself)

Down to the DNA

Al Carlucci

ISBN

Hardcover: 978-1-965560-62-4

Paperback: 978-1-965560-63-1

About the Author

I was born in a small town in Italy called Castel Pizzuto in the province of Campobasso. I came to Toronto Canada in 1957 only 6 months old with my parents on their pilgrimage for the American dream.

I grew up in North York, Toronto, in a middle class family where I went on to study music with world renown classical saxophonist "Paul Brodie", while studying jazz at York University, on my way to making a living as a jazz musician in the Toronto jazz circuit. This all came to a halt when I met the Lord God of Heaven and earth, in November of 1984, stopping me dead in my tracks!

I was so overwhelmed with this Divine encounter that tuned me into the reality of the Kingdom of God and all this *"forever stuff"*, that everything else became irrelative. This is where I started my slippery trek towards Heaven, while changing careers to carpentry according to the will of God for my life, which ushered in great stability and peace.

Up to this point in time (2010), I had not written anything, nor planned to. But as I continued to follow the Lord in His divine will for my life I found myself writing

4 books for the glory of God the Father. Who new?

I am now 67 years old on the threshold of *eternity*, and well on my way to the

City of the great King!

Email address:
albinocarlucci@icloud.com
albinocarlucci@hotmail.com

Phone Number: (647) 884-3676

Dedication

This book is dedicated everyone out there who desperately needs
to know how to totally empty and reload their bodies again!

Author's Note

It occurred to me one day as I was musing on the Word that in all My spirituality, I was still just another spiritual punk with too much knowledge! In the light of the Word of God (Psalms 119), I was just a professor of the Kingdom of God, not a possessor of the Kingdom, having a form of godliness, without the power, lacking the physical and Spiritual suffering, in the arena of Fasting, that is worthy of the glory of God!

Then I remembered when I first got saved, how, as a bride, I loved the Lord. I followed Him through the desert – through everything and anything. I was holiness unto the Lord; I would not dare let the holy flesh pass from Me! Yes, when the Lord broke My yoke, I said, "I would not stray away"! But on every high hill and under every green tree, I made love with sticks and stones. Overwhelmed with all those vain thoughts lodged in My head, all wrapped up in the cares and tares of this world. So, I decided to return to the Lord with all My heart in fasting, weeping, and mourning.

As the virgin (holy- clean) Daughter of Zion, that I AM.

Yes, Fasting is where I began to bring forth Fruit worthy of repentance. Hopefully, it will lead Me into weeping, then on to the burden of the Lord, and yes, even unto the Quickening of the Lord! My body, as the Temple of the Lord: must be clean-holy-set apart to the Lord. For the Holy Spirit needs a holy body to perfect the will of God in your life. The Christ in You is trying to manifest Himself through clean blood and a clean belly, (20 years of condiments, caffeine, and who knows what else) to develop a holy-eating lifestyle. My blood needs to be set apart for God. Jesus needs to be Lord of My food, which is a major and intimate part of life. So now, I sit under His shadow with great delight, His fruit being sweet to My taste, while I delight in the fatness of My soul, for I have eaten the

Duet. 32
pure blood of the Grape (communion).

It is impossible to maintain the Divine Design (Christ in You, the hope of glory) without a Fasted life, for the life of the soul and flesh are in the blood, and the only way to maintain clean (holy) blood for the life of Christ (the Divine Design) in your heart (holy blood) is by Fasting. The union of the Blood of Christ and your holy (clean) blood ushers in the reality of the Kingdom of God. The cleaner the blood, the greater the reality of God the Father. And the only way to clean the blood and the belly for the Temple of the Lord is by Fasting (the Wilderness)!

There is no other way.

Ps. 50
Gather My saints together unto Me, those who have made a Covenant with Me by sacrifice (Fasting?).

I believe that when a person is born again, his blood is quickened and cleansed for the entry of Christ in the heart; brand new heart and blood. That's why a man must be born again because a new life would require new blood, for the life of the flesh is in the Blood!

Joel 3: 21

I will cleanse Their blood that I have not cleansed:
For the Lord dwells in Zion (in the hearts of Believers).

Fasting has produced a resonance in My spirit that is right in tune with the holy Scriptures. I should have followed the Lord into Fasting (the Wilderness) when He first called me to Fast when I first got saved 20 years ago when He called me too Fast; what an enormous waste of time! This is where I went wrong. Most Christians reject this call of God for a New Wineskin, with new blood, for Your new Holy Spirit. The Lord will always lead a Born-again Christian into the Wilderness (Fasting) for a New Wineskin. As Born-again Christians, We have a new Spirit, but Our soul and flesh need much experience in the holy flesh and Holy Spirit!

Physical poverty (Fasting) for the sake of the Truth is Spiritual richness,
Even the Quickening of the Lord!

Table of Contents

Chapter 1

History of Fasting

Fasting and the Caveman!

In the days of old, Fasting was part of the Caveman's menu, for each day did not always provide food or a kill to eat. Sometimes, days without eating, and still not dying. Why? Because we are fearfully and wonderfully made in the image and likeness of the Heavenly Father. This Divine design would compensate for these intervals of Fasting, when there was no food or kill that day - or days, or weeks.

How does he manage to get up and out of his cave for the next kill? By the Father's Divine design in us!

Science tells us that after 18 hours into a Fast (of a clean Interior) - epinephrin up - adrenalin up - cortisones up - metabolic rate up because the Divine design is setting up an "intake mode" for survival for the next kill to eat. Or else he would just die in his cave. The Father has always looked after his children from the very beginning.

Science also tells us that after 3 days of Fasting the Immune system reboots itself.

But nowadays, this "intake mode" for survival has been stifled by the years of surfeiting (over-eating) with toxic available "processed foods" that are flooding the bloodstream like a river of death. This survival mode only works in a clean Interior like the cavemen had, for they were not bombarded with unnatural foods, so their Divine design could compensate for any deficiencies because of a clean Interior (Divine design).

A Faster Today would get opposite negative effects after 18 hours, not positive effects! It would take up to 10 Fasts to experience positive effects and feelings, because of the large amount of "toxic waste" being eliminated from the body and bloodstream and skin pores, which produces negative effects.

So until the body's "toxic waste level" comes down below 50%, there will be no positive effects, just the negative effects of toxic waste burning away from a lifetime of undigested meals gone bad and the intake of too much unnatural food going into your body.

Cavemen operated at a very low body "toxic waste level", therefore, in harmony with the man's Divine design.

The Faster must reduce his body's "toxic waste level" (first 10 -20 Fasts) to experience the full benefits of the Divine design. The Father will not allow just anybody to enter His realm of power. Fasting (and Prayer) can generate enough power to move a mountain (according to Jesus, who was raised from the dead). So, it must be tempered with all the humility that comes from Fasting. (Much more on toxic body waste up ahead).

The human body is designed to Fast and does most of its body repair during this time of Interior rest.

We do not need to eat 5 or 6 times a day. A person's body fat (energy) contains over 50,000 calories stored in the body, and it would take more than a month to run out of them and die. We are fearfully and wonderfully made beyond belief, and we can be safe and evolve into our Divine design as we wait for our new "Heavenly bodies" from above to dwell forever. (If we just listen to our bodies.)

DIET CHANGES THROUGH THE CENTURIES.

Man has evolved from the caveman days of a sparing diet with a clean Interior into the "Agriculture age" of plenty of rich and healthy food, up to the invention of the steel mill which brought flour, which ushered in many changes from the structure and authenticity of natural food.

And here we are now at the "Industrial age" of taking out processed foods and eating on the run, all day, every day.

This kind of worldly over-eating (surfeiting) can be dangerous to the Interior of Man, which started off so fearfully and wonderfully made as a Newborn baby. You should consider wisely before putting anything new in your mouth, and ask yourself if it is time and in line with my Divine design. (Is it processed or natural food?)

People lived long healthy lives before processed food came along.

Global Fasting

God, through His divine providence, has incorporated Fasting into the whole world for everyone. The word "Breakfast" speaks of the breaking of the Fast (break-fast), by not eating all night. In the morning, you break (the) fast. God has given everyone a small worldwide example for the maintenance of the interior, that man should be incorporating into his diet, even Fasting, the harness of God.

Behold, holy flesh and blood is required for the Temple of the Holy Ghost.

Everyone's belly needs this time of Fast through the evening for digestive resolve, and the balancing of the Interior of the body. Eating consumes a lot of energy - if you eat 100 calories, it takes 60 to 70 calories to digest those 100. So, the body and all its intricate workings, all at the same time, welcome this vacation of the Fast!

The body and the vital organs get rest during this time of Fast.

But in this modern age, more Fasting is required because of the high volume of food intake and the poor quality thereof. From Genesis to Revelation, we see food and the abstinence of it (Fasting) as a binding component in the Covenants of God. The eating and not eating of certain trees in the Garden, then the strict, holy dietary laws of Moses, then all the holy eating of the holy sacrifices by the Priests: the Last Supper, and finally the Marriage Supper of the Lamb.

Bread and Water of Life - the Lord's spiced Wine,
Fruit of the Spirit - milk and meat of the Word,
the Corn of Heaven – the Vine and Fig tree of the Lord etc.

Fat bones, goodly pastures, all the paths of the Lord dropping with fatness, making fat the soul: That Promised Land flowing with milk and honey; and again, in the End, to partake of the Tree of Life! The Last Supper was imperative before going to the cross as a testimony to the new Covenant. Food and abstinence play a vital role in the saint's Life. According to Acts 15:29, the 3 new Laws of the New Covenant are centered on food. Fasting will harmonize spirit, soul, and body for the full benefits of the Covenant-Kingdom life. Jacob would not bless Esau with the Covenant (his future) until there was a meal provided to eat, and He waited for it. Daniel, on the other hand, would not eat the king's meals, not wanting to defile himself. So, it appears to Me that food plays a vital role (both the eating and the non-eating of food) in Salvation.

FOOD LUST IS THE FOUNDATION OF ALL OTHER LUST. ALL THE OTHER LUSTS SPRING OUT OF THE HABITUAL FOOD LUST – FOR IT IS THE LUSTING OF THE SOUL

Remember how the Devil subverted the Father's divine design with just a piece of food? This is his #1 arsenal for the earth and mankind.

It took the devil a thousand years to kill Adam (even in His fallen state), because he had to first penetrate. His divine holy flesh, to get into the interior; His heart (blood), where the throne (will) sits. Fasting will forge the body, soul, and Spirit together as a whole (a whole heart), in unison with the Father. We need to eat the way God wants Us to eat, and when He tells us not to eat, which was the reason for the fall of Man.

Pro. 10
A fool's mouth is his destruction.

Ecc. 10
The lips of the fool will swallow him up.

But the Father of Mercies has restored Man to His original divine design through the Second Adam, who now dwells fearfully and wonderfully in the Inward Man (Christ in you) of "whomsoever will." God knows the exact condition of Your Interior, and you do not (how much excess, how much deficiency), and can balance the difference through the holy flesh (Fasting), The harness of God for Your life.

Pro. 21
He that keeps his mouth (food) and his tongue (words) preserves his life.

Pro. 15
A wholesome (tamed – Fasted)) tongue is a Tree of life, but perseveness in it breaks the spirit.

YOUR MOUTH WILL EITHER MAKE OR BREAK YOU!

(One way or another – sooner or later.)

Forced Famine

There was a forced famine (Fast) in the land whenever there was a major move of God. We see this pulling back of food supply with all the Patriarchs, and even Israel as a nation, in their captivities. Abraham, Isaac, and Jacob all had to go down to Egypt for food because of famine, and they all came back with great substance.

Israelites (Zion - the Church) straightway into the Wilderness (desert).
John the Baptist straightway into the Wilderness.
Jesus straightway into the Wilderness.
Paul straightway into the Wilderness.

David often in the Wilderness (Fasting).
Ezekiel with His forced unsavoury diet.

Where is your straightway into the Wilderness (Fasting)?

The Wilderness (Desert)

There are two kinds of wilderness:

1. Dry - unfruitful wilderness for the wicked – separation from God (Jer. 17:6),
2. Watered - fruitful Wilderness (in Christ) for the Righteous (Ps. 65:12).

In both cases, their a Wilderness, the idea of being alone and apart from the world.

For the Christian, it is separation from the flesh and the world when entering the Promised Land (Christ in You, the hope of glory). This is where God has Your attention, with no strength in the arm of the flesh, with no luxuries of the world, with no lusts of the flesh at all. God's wilderness has always been Fasting, to shut everything down for renovations, with the Interior ruling over the exterior.

Jer. 2
I remember Your devotion when You were young (first Born again), how as a bride You loved Me.
How You followed Me through the Wilderness, through a land not sown.
. . . where no man has passed through.

Ps.74
Jesus has broken the heads of the dragons (Devil and his bunch) in the waters (the soul):
He has broken the heads of the Leviathan in pieces,
and has given him to be meat for the People in the Wilderness (in Christ).

Ps.72
They that dwell in the Wilderness shall bow before Him, and His enemies shall lick the dust.

Ps.65
You crown the year with goodness and Your paths drop with fatness.
They drop upon the pastures of the Wilderness, and the little hills rejoice on every side.

Ps. 55

Oh, had I wings like a dove, I would fly away and be at rest.
Behold, then would I wander far off and remain the Wilderness (in Christ).

It is one thing to read your Bible and work labours of love on a fully loaded body, but doing the will of God after 20 days into the Wilderness (Fast) is an entirely different Ballgame.

It takes a mighty man (woman) of valour!

<u>*Because of your unbelief.*</u>

After 2-3 days -

unbelief is unimportant and little discerned.

After 4-6 days -

unbelief has made some impression.

After 8 days -

unbelief has made more impression and is being comprehended.

After 10 days -

unbelief is beginning to be realized.

After 14 days -

spiritual forces of all kinds are deeply recognized.

After 21 days

there has been a great spiritual shaking and a deep burden: Spiritual battles are at full force between the flesh and the spirit.

In a major Fast (hunger returns 30-50 days) through to victory, unbelief is totally exposed, and the Christ within is quickened to take over. The consecrated and yielded Servant may cast out the unbelief (whatever). No obstacle can be removed until we realize it is an obstruction, and become deeply burdened (Fasted) about the victory!

Mathew 17
Then Jesus said unto them, "because of your unbelief," for truly I say unto you,
If you have faith as a grain of mustard seed, and shall say to this mountain,
"Remove yourself from here to there," it shall be removed,
and nothing shall be impossible to you.

Howbeit this kind only comes out by prayer and Fasting.

Thank you Father for the burden of Zion,
and for the burden of Your word:
even the burden of the Lord

Chapter 2

Spiritual reasons for Fasting.

Fasting is one of the four foundations of the Christian faith; A major foundation that supports the Building (the Christ in You) of God. You do not want any major foundation missing from any structure.

Fasting coupled with Faith, inspires the mighty man - a woman of valour – the Servant of the Lord, to soar the high places (Divine revelations) of the earth to get a good look below.

Fasting and Faith both have the same weapon of warfare - the tongue.

(Jesus used His tongue as His only instrument of healing)

They both have the same goals, likes and dislikes.

Together, they are in perfect harmony working for You as your servants. So, do not have them sit down until You are done with them.

Fasting removes unbelief: it sees and reaches unbelief to cast it out.

Fasting produces a seriousness and a graveness in the soul and body, as a bedrock for the fear of the Lord: Faithfully and fearfully in the Way.

Nothing quickens the fear of the Lord like Fasting.

FASTING WILL SQUASH THE CONFIDENCE AND AGGRESSION OF THE OUTER MAN!

All the members of the powerful early Church Fasted. (Acts 14:23)

Paul was in Fasting's often, as the blueprint for true Discipleship. (2 Cor. 11:27)

Fasting breaks the yokes of sin, oppression, and everything else. (Isa.58)

Fasting produces Light – glory – and an answer from the Lord. (Isa. 58) - Fastest way to access the Blessings.

Fasting motivates and inspires the Inner Man with access to a deep understanding of the Wisdom of God.

Fasting retains a cross reference of the Word of God, which is alive, active, and sharp, dividing everything.

Fasting is the harness of God on your life maintaining clean blood for a whole heart, which retains the Word.

Fasting puts You into a slow mode which produces lowliness of mind and patience (in an excessively big way).

Fasting provides a climate for deep meditation (Feed) because of the slow mode.

Fasting produces the Burden of the Lord and His word because of the pouring out of your soul and body.

Fasting is the fastest way back home to God.

Fasting exposes the true nature of the outer man in his nakedness.

Fasting allows the Inner Man to feast and get strong! (when the outer stops eating the Inner Man feasts)

Fasting provides lots of Spiritual stamina!

Fasting always provides a sweet aroma of victory (just like Faith).

Fasting gives us an open invitation, and an arena for the fellowship of His sufferings, which is imperative for the power of His resurrection.

Fasting will keep us Wise and in the house of mourning, instead of being a fool by always being found in the house of myrrh (pleasure-flesh).

Fasting, by itself, without anything added to it, becomes a prayer of the highest Order.

No greater love has a man that he lay down his life down for his brother.

Fasting is mentioned one third as many times as prayer in the Bible.

Physical Reasons for Fasting

Fasting is the fastest way to squash any vice (3 -6 days)!

Fasting provides clean blood that is harmoniously conducive to the Holy Ghost.

Fasting improves blood circulation and brings on an automatic blood transfusion.

(Removing all clogs and chokes to the deepest levels.)

Fasting produces the holy flesh (Jer. 11) through the Circumcision of Christ (Col. 2)

"The life of the flesh and the soul is in the blood."

Fasting arrests the natural appetites, giving full Way to the Inner Man (quickly and dramatically flipping the natural to the Spiritual.)

Fasting will conserve and preserve energy for proper meditation.

Fasting gives Your whole body a vacation, while the vital parts get bathed in all the excess blood from the weight loss.

Fasting cleanses the intestinal tract to function at maximum efficiency.

Fasting will starve away disease, or anything unlike the Kingdom of God. (Only what is not needed is eradicated.)

Fasting will revitalize body glands: Your complexion with the glory of God (Moses's face).

Fasting removes bad taste buds from the mouth, turning the bitter to sweet. (appreciation for everything – especially the holy flesh)

Fasting will balance out over-eating or under-eating.

Fasting will give You an understanding of true and false hunger. (and the strength to go from true hunger to true hunger.)

Fasting sharpens the senses, especially the ears, to hear Him.

Fasting will add lots of years to Your life so that Your youth is renewed like the eagle.

Fasting makes new brain cells fast. The body produces a hormone that goes to the brain and tells your brain and tells your brain to switch on.

Fasting produces Growth hormones (the stuff that keeps you young) - .1 injection costs $400 – but 2 days of Fasting gets you a free 2000% more!

Fasting also rejuvenates blood cells.

Fasting is the fastest way to produce Stem Cells at no financial cost, which can be very expensive.

After Fasting food is metabolized much more forgivingly and efficiently than eating in a fed state.

The energy saved on Fasting is reutilized for body repair.

(All this information is well documented! Don't take my word for it, check it out yourself!)

Isa. 52
Awake, awake; put on your strength, O Zion, put on your beautiful garments oh Jerusalem, the holy City. For there shall no more come in unto You the uncircumcised and the unclean.

Shake Yourself from the dust; arise and sit down, O Jerusalem:
Loose Yourselves from the bands of Your neck, O captive Daughter of Zion.

Phil. 3
Whose end is their destruction, and whose god is their belly.

Food is the oldest and most subtle of all idols, since the Garden: it was the destruction of Man, and still is today! Satan did not come with fame or fortune but with food. The power of life and death being in the tongue (Pro. 18). Satan knows that if he can get a hold of your tongue, he can get a hold of your life.

Pro. 13
He who guards his mouth (food) and his tongue (words) preserves his life.

Pro. 20
Food won by fraud taste sweet, but later the mouth will be filled with gravel!

When the body is left to its Divine Design in a complete Fast (from true hunger till true hunger returns, 30-50 days), it will provide a total blood transfusion, vacationing and bathing the organs in all the excess blood due to lost weight, with a new-born baby's belly, gushing out some serious Living waters (Life of God)! Fasting cleanses the blood, and "the life of the flesh is in the blood." (Lev.11). This is what it is all about: His blood and the state of your blood, for a full Life from Above!

Jesus was born with the Blood of God, and You can't get any cleaner than that. His pure blood and Faith condemned sin in the flesh, and so will Yours, through Faith and the holy flesh (Fasting), even from deep unto Deep! Fasting is the gateway into the fellowship of His sufferings, that We might share in the power of His resurrection. No one likes the idea of suffering, but that is where all the glory is. The Holy Spirit needs a holy body to manifest Himself, which includes clean blood, a belly, and a Tamed tongue.

I AM: bought with a Price!

My body (holy flesh) and Spirit belong to God, but my soul is continually in my hand. The interior must be as clean as the Temple of the Lord. All the Ancients of the old had a Fasted, holy, eating lifestyle! John the Baptist came eating only locust and honey, His holy flesh as the microphone of Authority, as everyone came to him!

Ecc. 10
Woe to you, oh land (the heart) when your king (will) is a child (uncontrolled), and your princes look to eat in the morning. But blessed are You, oh Land (Christ in You), when Your king (will) is the son of nobles (trained by experience), and Your princes eat in due season, for strength and not for gluttony.

I have no right to eat whatever I want: Whenever I want, as much as I want; and long as I want.

Rm 16
For they that are such, serve not our Lord Jesus Christ, but their own bellies. (Watch for the bribes!

If Jesus is not Lord over Our food, then He is not Lord over a major and intimate part of Our lives.

Jesus wants to be God of our bellies so that the Living waters thereof may continue to flow, *"for the Lord sits as King upon the flood."*

All believers are supposed to Fast; Jesus said they shall Fast when the bridegroom is taken away, but no set rules or regulations are given as to how long, how often, or even the intricate specifics of Fasting.

The Father himself teaches the Faster the art of Fasting.

P.S.
A large amount of consistent willpower is needed to finish a Fast.

Chapter 3

Fearfully and Wonderfully made.

One day, as a teenager, our class went on a field trip to the Science Centre. They had a movie called the "Incredible Man" which I went to see. It was the most amazing and informational 40 minutes I ever spent. I was overwhelmed by all the different interconnections of everything all working at the same time. Each part of the body is absolutely amazing.

When it was time to leave, I hesitated in fear at the fact of standing up because of the understanding of all the working and tremendous pressure upon the foot in one step. It staggered my mind for a few seconds knowing how fearfully and wonderfully made we are! This was my very first encounter with the Heavenly Father ten years before I got Saved!

When investigating the human body, the first thing you will find is that the body, in all its complex and intricate work, has a Designer for this Heavenly divine design. The human body is too fearfully and wonderfully made to think that some random explosion in space – or something crawled out of the waters, could create such a beautiful, soft, complex being with a body, soul, and spirit to go with it.

Man is God's peculiar treasure, fearfully and wonderfully made.

We take our Divine Design for granted every day!

Here is just a few things on how fearfully and wonderfully made we are.

The Brain

Self-generating for up to 100 years.

Your brain's storage capacity is considered virtually unlimited.

Brain information travels up to an impressive 268 miles per hour.

You only use 10% of your brain capacity.

A piece of brain tissue the size of a grain of sand contains 100,000 neurons and 1 billion synapses.

The human brain can generate about 23 watts of power (enough to power a lightbulb).

The most complex manifestation of intelligence that we know of resides between our ears.

It takes only 2% dehydration to affect your attention, memory, and other cognitive skills.

Ninety minutes of sweating can temporarily shrink the brain as much as one year of aging.

The Word of God tells us that we (Christians) have the "Mind of Christ". (1 Cor. 2: 16) with all its treasures of wisdom and knowledge. (Col 2:3)

And much, much, more

Heart

Self-generating up to 100 years - strongest pump known to mankind.

Your heart beats over 100,000 times per day and is self-generating for up to 100 years

Your heart pumps about 1.5 gallons of blood every minute.

Over the course of a day, that adds up to over 2,000 gallons.

Other than the cornea, every cell in the human body gets blood from the heart.

The right side of your heart pumps blood into your lungs.

The left side of your heart pumps blood back through your body.

As amazing as the brain is, the Father has chosen the heart of man to dwell in.

The Word of God tells us that if we believe with our hearts, we can move mountains. (Mark 11:24)

And much, much more!

The Eyes

Your eyes focus on 50 different objects every second.

The only organ more complex than the eye is the brain.

Your eyes can distinguish approximately 10 million different colors.

80 percent of all learning comes through the eyes.

Your eyes can detect a candle flame 1.7 miles away.

Your iris (the colored part of your eye) has 256 unique characteristics; your fingerprint has just 40.

Only 1/6 of your eyeball is visible.

The average person blinks 12 times a minute.

Your eye is the fastest contracting muscle in the body, contracting in less than 1 / 100th of a second.

The optic nerve contains more than one million nerve cells.

The Word of Gods tells us that the eye is the light of body. (Mt. 6: 22)

And much, much more!

The Nose

Nasal mucous membrane color is an indicator of health. Pink indicates a healthy nasal mucous membrane, red signifies infection, and muted pink and gray can appear during nasal allergy season.

Smell is the only one of the five senses directly connected to the area of the brain where memories are formed and emotions are processed.

Your nose and sinuses produce almost one liter of mucus a day (which you typically don't notice and swallow). A single sneeze makes 40,000 droplets, travels up to 20 miles per hour, and creates a 5' spray radius.

You don't sneeze in your sleep because the nerves that trigger sneezing are also sleeping. Hungry? 80% of what you're tasting is determined by what you're smelling.

Your nose is lined with microscopic hair-like structures called cilia. Cilia sweep mucus to the back of the nose every five to eight minutes. Nasal cilia move up to 20 hours after death. Researchers believe this could measure the time of death.

There are 14 basic nose shapes.

Mucus contains chemicals that keep you healthy. Humans have about 12 million olfactory (smell) receptor cells, while rabbits have 100 million - bloodhounds have four billion.

And much, much more!

The Ears

Our sense of balance lies in our ears:

The hardest bone: the temporal bone, which protects the inner ear, is the hardest in the human body.

The smallest bone: the ear also houses the smallest bone in the body.

Our ears are always working: Did you know that our ears and hearing never rest? When we sleep, our brain is capable of ignoring sounds around us and only reacts to loud or unexpected noises as a defense mechanism.

The inner ear creates electric impulses.

The saving Faith of God comes through hearing and hearing by the Word of God. (Rm. 10: 17) And Faith can move a mountain!

And much, much more!

The Tongue

The tongue never gets tired. Regardless of how much people eat or talk. The tongue is also known for its flexibility. Tongues are so strong and flexible because they are made up of eight different muscles.

There are lots of taste buds up to 10,00 taste buds. Be aware that your taste buds die and get replaced every few weeks. People with thousands of taste buds are known as supertasters, while people with fewer taste buds are called non-tasters.

The tongue can taste everything. There are no divided areas on your tongue for tasting sour, sweet, or bitter tastes. Every area of your tongue can taste everything.

Your tongue is unique - Your tongue is unique. Your tongue is similar to a fingerprint. In the future, there is talk that tongues may be used as a type of identification method.

Your tongue is always working!

The Word of God tells us that the power of life and death is in the tongue. (Pro. 18: 20-21)

That a wholesome tongue is a Tree a Life. (Pro. 10: 11).

And much, much more!

The Hands

Self-lubricating your whole life - never able to duplicate fingerprints no two the same – brand new unique prints coming out on babies every day.

Our hand has 27 bones. The carpal or wrist accounts for 8; the metacarpal or palm has 5; the remaining 14 are digital bones, fingers, and thumb. Our hands have 29 major joints, at least 123 ligaments, 34 muscles, 48 nerves, and 30 arteries.

There are no muscles in our fingers. Our fingers can move because of the muscles located in the palm and in the middle of the forearm. They're connected to our finger bones by tendons which pull and move our fingers like the strings of puppet.

What sets our hands apart from other animals is our opposable thumbs – means our thumbs and fingers can work together. Our fingers are more sensitive than our eyes. fingertips have receptors responsible for sending messages to the brain. Venna Amoris, the vein on our ring finger has a direct line to our heart. That's why we wear the engagement ring on the left hand's finger because it is also known as the Vein of love.

Motor Cortex is the part of our brain that controls all movements in our body and about a quarter is devoted to the muscles in our hands.

Indeed, our hand is one of the most complex and fascinating pieces of natural engineering in the entire human body. There is nothing close to replacing our hands' usefulness and adaptability. That is why it's so difficult to imagine how much our lives will be affected without it.

The Feet

One-quarter of your body's bones are in your feet. Each normal foot has 33 joints, 26 bones, 19 muscles, and 107 ligaments.

The skin on the soles of your feet is thicker than it is anywhere else on the human body.

Each foot has more than 250,000 sweat glands, and they can produce up to half a pint of moisture a day!

Walking is the best exercise for your feet, and it's also a great way to get overall exercise for your body: it boosts circulation and helps you burn calories.

Standing still is much more tiring than walking. Your body only uses a few specific muscles when you're still, whereas walking distributes the weight and effort over more muscles. Your feet may be the most ticklish part of your body. This is because we have 8,000 nerves in our feet.

The Belly

The acid in your belly is strong enough to burn your skin.

When empty, the stomach is pretty small – it is only about the size of your fist. However, it is also capable of stretching to hold up to 4 liters of food – equal to about 8 tubs of Ben & Jerry's ice cream!

The acid in our stomach is strong enough to digest most of the organs in the body. It is even strong enough to dissolve some metals!

The stomach is the only organ in the digestive system that has three layers of muscles.

The stomach is like a small chemical factory.

The average length of the intestines is about 26 ft. - with a range of 21 to 30 ft.

The total surface area of your intestines is about half the size of a Paddington court.

You do not have to go past your nose to see God, for. We are made in the likeness (outside) and image (inside) of the Father. There are all kinds of evidences all over the world and space that all declare His glory.

We must be faithful and grateful for all these amazing simultaneous workings (both inner and outer) of our fearful and wonderful creations by Fasting for the maintenance of the body (belly) and blood. The blood is supreme in the body.

A person can stay alive with any part of his body missing except the blood. The blood infiltrates every part of the body, replenishing every part, nook, and cranny, including cells. So, it is vital to the performance of your life to maintain the blood by the regeneration of Fasting.

You (your feelings - thoughts – imagination – senses) are the state of your blood!

Lev. 17:11
The life of the flesh (and soul) are in the blood.

The Blood

It's red and you need it. That's what people know about the most valuable substance in the world. Your blood keeps you alive, and without the blood, nothing would get to where it needs to be. The blood is the roads and highways of the Interior body.

Blood brings oxygen to your cells and removes waste products, functions you cannot live without.

Most of your blood consists of water. In spite of this, however, there is no way to create blood artificially. It is completely up to our bodies to create the blood. The red blood cells start their life in the bones (marrow), and after muting for 7 days, they are released into the bloodstream to begin their important duties.

Each blood cell will make a complete cycle (100,00 miles) through your body in just about 30 seconds because of the relentless pumping of your heart.

Each blood cell will continue to circulate for 100 days before it dies and is replaced with a new one.

It is amazing how your body works together to keep you alive.

A few facts about blood.

Self-generating up to 100 years

Your body has over 100,000 miles of blood vessels, which, if laid end to end, would stretch 2 and a half times around the Earth.

Blood carries the following to the body tissues: Nourishment – Electrolytes – Hormones – Vitamins – Antibodies – Heat – Oxygen.

Blood carries the following away from the body tissues: Waste matter. - Carbon dioxide

In an average lifetime, the human heart pumps 1.5 million barrels of blood (that's enough to fill 200 train tank cars).

One unit of blood can be separated into several components: red blood cells, plasma, platelets and cryoprecipitate.

A red blood cell is around 7 microns in size. (A micron is one-millionth of a meter).

It only takes 20 to 60 seconds for a drop of blood to travel from the heart, through your body, and back to the heart again.

Each red blood cell has 270,000,000 hemoglobin molecules; each hemoglobin molecule can carry four oxygen molecules.

The circulatory system in the human body stretches 66,000 miles, more than two and a half times the circumference of the Earth.

The heart beats 2.5 billion times during the life of a 75-year-old.

There are 150 billion red blood cells in one ounce of blood - There are 2.4 trillion red blood cells in one pint of blood.

The human body manufactures 17 million red blood cells per second. If stress precipitates a need, the body can produce up to 7 times that amount. (That's up to 119 million red blood cells per second.)

The heart expels 2 ounces of blood with each beat, five quarts of blood each minute, 220 million quarts in 70 years.

Red blood cells (erythrocytes) are the body's cellular lungs; their job is to ferry oxygen to every cell and remove carbon dioxide.

The hemoglobin in red blood cells scoops up oxygen molecules in oxygen-rich tissues such as the lungs and then releases them in oxygen-deprived tissues throughout the body (throughout the day – throughout the year – throughout decades)

If the red blood cells from one person were to be stacked in the sky, they would reach 31,000 miles. Each second, we lose about 3 million red blood cells only to be replaced by the same number produced in the bone marrow. Venous blood that delivers carbon dioxide back to the lungs makes up 75 percent of blood flow at any given moment.

White blood cells: Help heal wounds. They do this by fighting infection, and also by taking in matter, such as dead cells, tissue debris, and old red blood cells. Are our protection from foreign bodies that enter the blood, such as allergens?

Help to protect against changed (mutated) cells, such as cancer.

Those strange bright white dots you see floating around when you look at the sky are white blood cells.

Fasting is the fastest and purest way to renew and cleanse your blood.

A newborn baby has about one cup of blood in his body.

There are about 2 mg of gold in your bloodstream.

We can now understand how vital the blood is, and how vital the maintenance of it is. Nothing gets done or gets anywhere without the blood, and Fasting is the only way to naturally cleanse and renew your blood and body. The blood is supreme overall. We cannot live without it. Even with no heart or brain, science can keep you alive. But they cannot keep anybody alive without the right amount of blood.

We should try and maintain our body and blood for maximum performance by regular Fasting to give our vital organs a vacation from all the amazing, intricate, simultaneous, inner workings of the Divine design. Remember that the life of the soul is also in the blood. Your feelings, thoughts, imagination, willpower, and Spiritual potential are in the blood. The better the blood, the better everything else.

Man's eternal salvation comes through the heart. The most important thing in your life (after God) should be the state of your blood, which keeps you alive, how to empty and reload your body and blood, and how often to do it (at least 4 major Fasts a year). Most people have never reloaded their blood and body before. The Blood is the main reason we Fast.

Have you ever totally emptied your body and blood before? Then, reloaded them again!

You cannot put a price on that!

Spiritual Blood

Christians are blessed with access to two types of blood. Their own blood of their Divine design and the spiritual Blood of the Lamb of God (Jesus) that takes away the sin of the world. It is impossible to maintain the Divine Design (Christ in You, the hope of glory) without some kind of Fasted life, for the life of the soul and flesh is in the blood. The only way to maintain clean (holy) blood for the life of Christ (the Divine Design) in your heart (holy blood), is by Fasting.

Clean blood = clean God-life (holy Flesh).

Adam had the blood of God until the fall tainted His blood to this day. His fall from the God-life passed down tainted blood from generation to generation. Therefore, all born from him would have tainted blood (separation from God) and need to be Born again (new Blood) for the Life (blood) of God. The Bible tells us that by one man's (Adam) offense (disobedience – the Fall), death (tainted blood – separation from the Father) entered into this world upon all men: so, by one Man's (Jesus) obedience (righteousness clean blood – Life of God) came upon all men who Believe. For the Blood of Jesus cleanses us from all unrighteousness, even our blood (1Jn. 1).

Blood of Jesus cleanses Us from anything, anywhere, anytime, forever

It is the union of the Blood of Christ and your holy blood that ushers in the reality of the Kingdom of God.

And the only way to clean the blood and the belly for the Temple of the Lord is by Fasting (the Wilderness)!

There is no other way.

Ps. 50:5
Gather My saints together unto Me, those who have made a Covenant with Me by sacrifice (Blood - Fasting).

I believe that when a person is Born Again, his blood is quickened (made alive unto God) for the entry of Christ in the heart; Brand new heart and blood. That's why a man must be Born Again because a new life would require new blood, for the life of the flesh is in the Blood!

Joel 3: 21
I will cleanse Their blood that I have not cleansed:
For the Lord dwells in Zion (the hearts – clean blood of Believers).

Chapter 4

New Wineskins

(New body - blood - belly.)

Pro. 14
A sound heart (clean blood) is the life of the flesh (holy flesh).

It stands to reason that the Holy Spirit would require holy Flesh (body), with a holy soul (the mind – knowledge – feelings, emotions)! It is imperative that the flesh be holy, for the Lord is holy! The body is the house of God's Divine design (Christ in you, the hope of glory), and it must be holy, for God is holy, He reigns upon the throne of His holiness, and so should You.

Eze. 43
This is the Law of the House of God: upon the top of the mountain, and all the land around it, will be most holy (which definitely includes eating). Behold, this is the law of the House.

1 Cor. 3:16
Do you not know that you are the Temple of God, and that the Spirit of God dwells in you? If any man defiles the Temple of God, him shall God destroy, for the temple of God is holy, which temple you are.

So, the Holy Spirit requires a holy body (the Temple). Jesus speaking on Fasting refers to new Wineskins. Jesus said that His new Wine (Holy Spirit) must be put into new Wineskins (bodies); therefore, the new Wineskin (through the Circumcision of Christ) has the potential to bear the stature of Christ – "for as He is, so are We in this world."

Our bodies (through Fasting) need to be able to also bear the full load of the burden of the Word, and the burden of Zion into new Wineskins, for out of your belly will flow rivers of Living waters. There are many daily distractions and pollution choking the body through various avenues, the mouth (food) and tongue (words) being the highways thereof, for the power of life and death are in the tongue.

Jn. 6
He who believes on Me, as it is written, out of his belly will flow rivers of Living waters.

These rivers of Living waters flow from your belly, not your heart nor your head, implying the belly (clean blood and body) is the source of the Living waters. Fasting is the best and quickest way to get them out. Fasting totally shuts down the flesh and cleans the blood, giving Way to the inward Man. We need to focus on our belly's more than our heads.

God wants our interior and blood refined to pure holiness
unspotted from the flesh, and the world, for the pure blessing!

This is the main reason for the lack of power in the Body of Christ. Most Christians are so busy with their souls that they forget all about their bodies, which is the Spirit's last stop for the expression of God's power in the world. The exterior needs to be established before the interior to make way for the Holy Spirit. When it comes to consecration (setting yourself apart from God), the holy flesh (Fasting) is the foundation of the Christ in You!

Pro. 24
I will prepare My work without (the holy flesh), and make it fit for the field (My heart):
then afterwards, I will build My palace.

Pro. 14
A Wise woman builds her mansion: but the foolish plucks it down with their hands.

God has given You a new Spirit, and now it is up to you to provide a new body (through Fasting and the Circumcision of Christ) and a new soul (through the Word), even Christ in You, the hope of glory. It's interesting to note that God demanded the plumbing of the sacrificial animals on the altar to be burned, the interior being dedicated to the Lord to be burned by the fire (Holy Ghost) of God.

Lev. 3
All the fat is mine, says the Lord.

Clean belly = clean blood = Holy Flesh = Holy Temple = Holy Life = power, joy, and great peace with the Father's presence!

Fasting is God's provision for the Holy Flesh and the Circumcision of Christ.

Isa. 4
The Lord will wash away the filth of the Daughters of Zion, and purge the bloodshed (guilt) of Jerusalem from
the midst thereof, by the Spirit of Judgment and by the Spirit of Burning (Fasting).

It is interesting to note that the Levites were on a fixed diet supplied by the holy offerings and sacrifices of God. Israel was to eat what was supplied according to the dietary Law of Moses, by the hand of Israel. Jesus wants full control of our mouths so that He can curb our appetites, words, and desires from the carnal to the Divine. He wants to Feed us with food that is that is convenient for us according to His will, maintaining the holy flesh, so that We do not get full and deny him.

Jer. 11
Therefore, I will not let the holy flesh (clean blood) pass from me. (Because My flesh trembles at Your word.)

Pro. 14
A sound heart (clean blood) is the life of the flesh (holy flesh),

Fasting - The Harness of God

Jer. 5
So, I went to the great men, and spoke to them, for they have known the way of the Lord, and the judgements of their God: but they have altogether broken the yoke (holy flesh) and taken off the harness (Fasting).

Most Christians serve the Lord in their own way, to fit their own lifestyle, without the holy flesh (it's expensive). Taming the mouth and the tongue is a lot of hard work. The so-called spiritual big shots had taken off the harness (a Fasted life), filling themselves up with the just deserts of their own lives. Fasting locks in the body and soul into the Spiritual with an undivided attention and holy drive, for a whole season!

Ps. 69
I chastened my soul with fasting, which is to my reproach, and my prayer returned into my own bosom.

Zech. 8:9
Thus, says the Lord of Hosts, The Fast of the 4th month and the fast of the 5th month, and the fast of the 7th month and the fast of the 10th month, shall be to the House of Judah joy and gladness, and cheerful feasts, therefore, love truth and peace (Trading food for the thick presence of the Lord. Everyone looked forward to the Feast of the Fast).

Fasting is the harness of God for the flesh, which fortifies the will to establish a throne (heart) of judgment in your life. This harness gives God and you much more control because the flesh and the world are not in the picture anymore. You are resolved, and when deep in the Fast, the voice of the enemy is very faint, if at all.

Ps. 119
This is my comfort in my affliction (Fasting), Your word has quickened me.

You'll be looking forward to the next Fast as soon as you reload your body and blood (with live, clean food). Fasting is a great, exciting holy Work and the high calling of God for all the Prisoners of Christ! This harness of Fasting will also flip your soul so that your physical feelings line up with the desires of the Spirit instead of the desires of your flesh: for when the flesh is weak (in its demands) by the discipline of the Fast, then, the Spirit be always willing.

Pro. 27
The full soul despises the Honeycomb (the Word), but to the hungry soul (humbled and disciplined through Fasting) every bitter thing is sweet.

Turning duty into delight,
turning the righteous into the upright,
turning the upright into the Just, and the Just into Christ,
with a readiness (insatiable) to avenge all disobedience!

Ps. 141
I will not eat the bread of wickedness, nor drink the wine of violence!

When you sit down to eat as lord over your own food, of which the Lord has no part, you will stray to the dainty bribes, and deceptive meat of the wicked Ruler (flippant, reckless eating - at Your command - fast food that is dedicated to idols). This eating lifestyle (little foxes) spoils the body and the blood, with the lust thereof spilling over into the soul. So, it is better to put a Knife (the Word – a meditation) to your throat, than to give in to his appetites. Consider this very carefully when You sit down to eat, or rise up to speak.

Ecc. 10
For the lips of the fool will swallow him up.

Pro. 23
Eat not the bread of him (the Devil - flesh) that has an evil eye: neither desire his dainty meats.

The food schedule that the devil has planned for you (by your thoughts and feelings), and by hastiness (lusting) and altered appetites are deceptive meat. If he can get the mouth out of control, the body, blood, and everything else will follow, and You will not even realize it.

Pro. 23
For as he thinks in his heart, so he is;
Eat and drink, he (devil-flesh) says to you; but his heart is not with you.
The morsel which you have eaten you will vomit up and lose your sweet (anointed) Words.

I have, in the past, when deep in a Fast turned hostile over a morning coffee, and I have also denied the Lord for a chocolate bar on a Fast. Imagine that? Maybe worse than Peter: but here I AM.

Pro.29
A king (over his soul and body) establishes the land (Christ in You) by judgment (His inheritance in Christ Jesus); but he that receives bribes destroys it.

The desires for God and pure feelings are expressed in the holy flesh and in labours of love, not in much studying and idle talk. The more holy the flesh, the more constant and intense the delight in the law of the Lord. When the flesh is weak (unclean), the Spirit will always lead into a Fast.

Pro. 16
The divine sentence is on my lips therefore, my mouth shall not transgress in judgment.

When you stop eating food, the inward Man will enjoy His meat and "fresh" Manna from Heaven, with the Lord's special, blended, spiced Wine, crushed from "pure blood of the Grape."

Pro, 24
I do eat Honey (the Word) because it is good, and the Honeycomb, which is sweet to my taste, and so is the knowledge of Wisdom to my soul.
When I find it (Wisdom) there's a reward, and my expectation soars.

Fasting boldly bites into the sweetness of Life that ushers in the knowledge of Wisdom, which is what your soul truly desires: to undo the heavy burdens, to let the oppressed go free, and you break every yoke. Fasting expands your horizon so that you may be able to "soar the high places of the earth, to search out the treasures of darkness, and the riches of secret places." Fasting is the bread of affliction (chastening) by a holy personal choice and is necessary before entering the Land of Milk and Honey! Jesus ate the bread of affliction served to Him from the Father's hand in the wilderness, and in the garden, and on the cross. Just like Israel in the desert!

The Born-again Christian cannot go forward and bear Fruit in Christ without some kind of a Fasted (chastened- pruned) life.

Jn. 15
Every branch that does not bear fruit will be cut down and taken away.

No pain! No Gain!

FASTING = SUFFERING = HUMILITY (appreciation) = GLORY

Fasting is the arena of suffering, forging the will of God on the will of your life, as the harness of God, binding Your flesh to God's altar of humility, minute by minute, hour by hour, and day by day from faith to faith, and from glory to glory!

1 Pt. 4
For as much then as Christ has suffered in the flesh, arm yourselves likewise with the same mind, for he who has suffered in the flesh has ceased from sin.

Rm. 6
If we be planted in the likeness of His death, we will also be in the likeness of His resurrection.

Planted how? In the suffering of Fasting, which is a holy suffering en route to the power of His resurrection. It is a glorious suffering loaded with every Spiritual blessing in Christ. Fasting will quickly build up your capacity for resistance, seeing that You are resisting temptation all day long, sometimes from minute to minute and hour to hour for days in a season of Fasting. For the most part, winning most small battles as a skilled Swordsman in the arena of Fasting, fighting the good fight of faith, together with the Sword of the Lord, the Word of His power, and Jesus, the Captain of our Faith (Fasting) training our hands for war (in Love – Christ) and our fingers to fight. The shock of the Fast on your flesh is most humbling, indeed, which will lift you up higher than you ever imagined.

Fasting compounds the fear of the Lord as a fountain of Life. Increasing the Fear of God in the many decisions of resistance to the temptation of food (or whatever).

By the minute, sometimes, strengthening the muscle of Faith, sharpening the Sword of the Spirit, and forging the will as a rod of iron in Your soul, each time Wiser (stronger) and Wiser (stronger). This iron will from Fasting also spills over into every aspect of one's life. Fasting also acts as a harness on the tongue, for in your weakness, you do a lot less talking, and much more meditating. (Speaking and listening to the songs of fools can be a chore at times!)

Ps. 12
May the Lord cut off all flattering lips, and the tongue that speaks proud things.
Who have said in their heart, "with our tongues we will prevail,
our lips are our own; who is Lord over us?

The fool folds his hands (Faith) and eats his own flesh (Life of God).

He eats up (squanders) his inheritance by putting aside the major foundation of Fasting (the holy flesh) that is dedicated to God as a living sacrifice, and by a flippant, worldly, selfish eating lifestyle filled with lust, spilling over as a catalyst into other lusts. The livelihood of their substance (holy flesh) eaten up: master over their own food – whenever – whatever - as much as they want. Eating like the world eats, that is dedicated to idols (Tim Hortons – McDonald's) filling them with the world. The lust of the eyes always being in the driver's seat, in a rush, and never satisfied,

WITH NO CONCEPT OF TRUE OR FALSE HUNGER, OR ANY RESTRAINT.

1 Cor. 6
Meats for the belly, and the belly for meat, but God shall destroy both. (ouch!)

Fasting curbs desires from the root (food) up! Food being the basest, greatest physical need and desire of the flesh and world. Jesus wants to feed us with food that is convenient (eating and Fasting) for us and not to stray and take off the harness. (My harness is four major Fasts per year, plus small ones in between.) If you take off God's harness of Fasting, you will lose control of your flesh, then Your soul, then Your Spiritual desires, which leads to the shipwreck of your Faith. An empty, powerless Christian life, alienated from the commonwealth of Israel, a stranger to the Land of Promise, wandering aimlessly in the flesh and the world, without God, and without hope in death!

Jesus wants to be Lord of Our bellies!

Fasting will bring a person into a deep and intimate relationship with his body, locking in the consciousness of food intake, monitoring the food intake, allowing ample time for the digestive resolve of the last meal (true hunger), and always knowing where you are from zero ground (Fast exit), which = a Fasted life.

What I eat, how much I eat, how often, considering the lust that is set before Me?

A BRIDLED BELLY = A BRIDLE TONGUE = BRIDLE LIFE = THE ANOINTING MOST OF THE TIME!

Chapter 5

The Spiritual Feed

There are two kinds of Spiritual Feeds:

1.

The feed of this world's (spirit of mammon and the flesh) Table, with all its dainties and tender morsels of lies and half-truths that will feed you with everything except Divine food, the Bread and Water of Life. This driving Feed of the world is carnal and mixed with the "bread of wickedness and the wine of violence." Definitely not for Me!

2.

Then there's the Feed of God, which is the Word of God, which is the Bread (Word) and Water (Holy Ghost) of Life.

The Lord's Table is always prepared with the finest of Wheat (the Word) and the Honey from the Rock, to be washed down with Living waters - the Lord promised spiced Wine (Holy Ghost), made from the pure blood of the Grape (Jesus), that makes glad the heart of the New Creature (Me - Child of God – half man, half God). Only the Bread and Water of Life can satisfy the "hidden Man of the heart," the Christ in You - Your hope of glory. There is a mountainous difference between a daily reading schedule and a daily Feeding schedule.

The difference is the Word made flesh, with the intake of the Bread of Life, and the proper digestion of it to the New Man. When the outer man stops eating, the belly and blood become clean – holy, set apart for the divine Design. Then the Inner Man starts Eating and flourishing because of the holy flesh, for the Holy Spirit needs a holy Body to dwell in, which unlocks every Spiritual blessing in Christ Jesus, in You.

It is the Father's good pleasure to invite everyone that thirsts to the Waters of God: and he that has no money to come, and buy (by Fasting) Wine and Milk without price – instead of spending money on that which is not Bread (Life), and labor (eat) for that which does not satisfy. He wants "whomsoever wills" to hearken diligently unto Him and to Eat that which is Good, as the soul delights itself in fatness (peace and joy) through Fasting, the Table of the Lord.

The Father wants the exterior and Interior of His peculiar treasures to believe in His divine Design. This is Our part (consecration), by Fasting and holiness (believing) in His sanctification (Divine Design). This is the Father's divine Design for the Church of the New Covenant, for "whomsoever will". Below is the Father's divine Design for the Church (the Bride of Christ – the Body of Christ). The fullness of all that fills all in all, a world without end!

Ps. 45

The Kings daughter (Body of Christ –the Church) all glorious within!

In pearls and gold embroidery will She be brought unto the King, in raiment (a dazzling wedding dress) of Needlework (fulfilled testing's of God): the virgin companions (true saints in the holy flesh) also that follow Her will be brought unto the King (Jesus); moving into the Kings palace with gladness and rejoicing.

Your sons shall step into your fathers' place and rise to be princes in all the earth. Carrying Your name on from age to age, till nations praise You forever and ever.

Jer. 17

A glorious high throne, from the beginning, is the place of Our Sanctuary (the Church – Zion – Body of Christ).

The Lord God is awesome out of His holy places (saints with holy flesh). The God of Israel is He that gives strength (New Interior through Fasting) and power to His people. The reality of this New Creation (Your Spiritual Inheritance) comes through the Spirit of holiness (holy flesh), which is the Law of the House!

Once again,

Jer.31

For the Lord has done a new thing in the earth.
A Woman with the strength of a Man (Christ in You).
(And a Man with the meekness of a Woman - Daughter of Zion).

This New Creature (2 Cor. 5:17), the Christ in You, has the characteristics of Solomon's simple, delicate, intricate, and Spiritual beauty of the Bride (Body of Christ), coupled together with the strength and confidence of the inward Man, that "Christ in You, the hope of glory," that ravishes even the heart of the Bridegroom, for We are fearfully and wonderfully made in Christ Jesus!

Ps. 119

Your hands have made me and fashioned me (Fasting – holy flesh), give me understanding that I may learn Your commandments.

The Bread of Life!

Jn. 6
I AM: the Bread of Life.
He who comes to Me will never hunger,
and he who believes in Me will never thirst.

This promise that My children will never hunger in their soul or thirst in their Spirit is refreshing and eternal to Me. All we have to do is bring the Children to Him (the Word) and do the work of the Word (keeping it - believing). Bringing the Children to Him (the Word) – daily and faithfully to be Fed: so that Their innocent heart may believe: to taste, and see that the Lord (Word) is good; and that He does satisfy with the finest of Wheat, and with the Honey from the Rock. God the Father wants the souls of His children fat, with joy and willpower, for the paths of the Lord drop with fatness, and the valleys are covered with Corn (the Word).

The Spiritual Diet

Finest of Wheat	for Wisdom and Spiritual understanding.
Milk and Butter	that They may know to refuse the evil, and choose the good.
Corn of Heaven	for holiness and labors of Love.
Honey	for the joy of the Lord.
Meat of His word	for strength and healing.
Wine of God	for the Anointing that breaks every yoke –

And much more of every kind, both new and old!

Feeding the children the Word (Bread of Life) of God is clothing their inner Man with Christ (His personality and His power), for the Lord and His name (Word) are One.

Rev. 11
"For He is dressed in a robe dipped in blood and His name is called the Word of God."

The Word became flesh with Jesus, and God wants the same for you ("Whosoever will").

A lot of adult-baby Christians have died through the ages by unconsciously starving their inner Man to death trying to strengthen themselves in their own iniquity (a lifestyle without God or the Bread of Life!). You do not want the Children growing up wasting all their time, and energy on the meat that perishes, but rather for the Meat that endures unto everlasting life, for they are certainly taking nothing with them when they leave this planet. The Meat of God will deliver their soul from death and keep them alive in times of famine, to do the will of Him who sent them and to finish His work. When the Spiritual Feed (the Word) begins, it automatically sets you apart for the Lord,

Ps. 4
For the Lord sets apart him who is Godly (Wordily) for Himself.

You become personally His, as the Word (Jesus) becomes personally Yours.

Inner Man verses the outer man!

This Bread of Life needs to come unto the Children.

Even the Word of God, which has been hiding for ages and generations but is now made known to His children, that is, Christ in Them, the hope of glory! The Father has provided exceeding great and precious promises (Seeds) for the Children to be partakers of His divine nature.

Milk for babes - Bread for the hungry - Meat for the strong - Honey for desert - Laver to cleanse -

Gold to enrich - Lamp to guide - Hammer to convict - Sword to attack - Fire to refine

Rain and Snow to refresh - Mirror to reflect - Bow for revenge

Seed to multiply - Power to create faith and eternal life.

For the Bread of Life in Them is alive and active, quick and powerful, sharper than any two-edged sword. It will divide their body, soul, and spirit from the crooked and quicken them to keep the law of their Mother (the Law of the Spirit of Life in Christ Jesus) and the Father's commandment. Then Spiritual feeding of the Children is much more complicated than the natural feed! The natural feed deals with physical food: they're fed and you're done with the seen outer man. But the Spiritual feed deals with the soul and spirit through the Word (Spirit) of God, the unseen – the inner Man.

This hiding (meditating) of the Word in the heart is a major part of the Feeding process of the inward Man – the Christ in Them, the hope of glory: that They sin not.

Ps. 119
I have hidden (treasured) Your word in my heart, so that I sin not against You.

This interaction of the outer man with the inward Man, through the confession - meditation of the Word subdues and resolves the aggression of the outer man through a constant, daily Feed of the Bread of Life. You want the Childs' "hidden Man of the heart" to be in control, rather than the carnal mind of the outer man, which only leads to death.

Pro. 18
The power of Life and death is in the tongue, and they that love it will (can) eat the fruit of it.

(These meds will provide a volume of Feed that outweighs the volume of the flesh and warfare. You now have plenty of downtime to memorize and meditate (Eat).)

FASTING - Meditation #2 - Bread of Life

Theme

Rev. 10:9

I went up to the angel, and said to him, give Me the little Book.
And he said to Me, take it and Eat it up;
It will make Your belly bitter, but in Your mouth sweet as honey.

Jer. 15:16

Father, I found Your words and did Eat them; They are unto Me a joy and
rejoicing in My heart; (a strength and a strengthening in My soul,
and a filling and a fulfilling in My body)

Job 23:12

Oh Jesus, I have esteemed the Words of Your mouth more than My necessary food.
Feed Me with food that is convenient for Me, lest I be full and deny You!

Mt. 4:4

Therefore, I do not live by the Word of God alone,
but by food also. (Holy Ghost Version.)

Introduction

Eph. 4:24

I AM: putting on the New Man (by the Bread of Life)
which after God
is created in Righteousness and true holiness.

1 Cor. 6:19-20

My body is the Temple of the Holy Ghost, which is in Me;
My body is no longer Mine.

I AM: bought with a Price, therefore, I will glorify God
with My body and My Spirit, which belongs to God.

Ps. 119:

For Your hands are making Me, and fashioning Me.

2 Cor.4:16

For which cause, I faint not: for though the outward man perish.
My inward Man (Christ in Me) is renewed day by day.

Ps. 139:14

I AM: Fearfully and wonderfully made!

Content

Pro. 9:1-2,5

Wisdom has built Her mansion, and set up Her seven pillars,
Her beasts are slain, Her wines are blended,
Her table is prepared:
Come, eat of My Bread, and drink of My Wine, says the Lord.

Jn. 6:35

Jesus is My Bread of life:
I will continue to come to Him; therefore, I will not hunger!
I will continue to believe in Him; therefore, I will not thirst!

Ps. 107:9

For He satisfies My longing soul and fills My hungry soul with goodness.

S.O.S 8::2

He also gives Me spiced Wine (Holy Spirit) to drink,
even the Nectar (the anointing) of His pomegranates.

Isa. 7:15

I do eat Butter and Honey (the Word), that I may know
to refuse the evil and choose the good.

S.O.S 2:3

I also sit under His shadow with great delight
and His fruit is sweet unto My taste.

Ps. 81:16

Jesus feeds Me with the finest of Wheat (the Word) and
with the Honey out of the Rock does He satisfy Me.

Mt. 5:6

For I hunger and thirst (all the time) for righteousness to the filling.

Pro. 28:25

My soul also is made fat because I always put My trust in the Lord.

Jn. 6:27

Therefore, I will not labor for the meat that perishes,
but for the Meat which endures unto everlasting life.

Ps. 63:5

now, is My soul satisfied as with marrow and fatness.

Ps. 33:18-19

Behold, the eye of the Lord is upon Me because I fear Him,
and I hope in His mercy; He delivers My soul from
death and keeps Me alive in time of famine.

Pro. 13:25

So then, I, as the righteous, do Eat (meditate) to the satisfying of My soul.

Ps. 16:9

Therefore, My heart (spirit) is glad, My glory (soul) rejoices:
and My body also rests in hope!

Thank you Father for the Bread of Presence (the Word) and the bread of affliction.
Let Me taste and see that the Lord is good!

Summary

1 Pt. 4:

Even as Christ has suffered in the flesh, I also arm Myself with the same Mind,
for if I suffer in the flesh, I will cease from sin.

Phil. 3:21

According to the working of His power, whereby He is able to subdue
all things (including Me) unto Himself.

Rm.13:14

I AM:
Putting on the Lord Jesus Christ (by the Word of His power);
I will make no provision for the flesh and its lusts.

Jn. 4:34

My meat is to do the will of Him who sent me and to finish His work.

P.S.

Pro. 16:10

The Divine sentence (the Word) is on My lips as king (over My soul and body);
My mouth will not transgress in judgment.

Duet. 32:14

For I have eaten the "pure blood of the Grape (Jesus).

Chapter 6

Entering the Fast

Target Focus
There are 3 holy targets to consider when Fasting
(Plus, whatsoever things you ask.)

The 1st

The Bread of Life - The Word of His Power

Which will Feed you when your mind starts wandering and craving any kind of deceptive meat that robs your soul and body of its holy (healthy) flesh, which contains your Inheritance of God.

(At the end of this chapter are meditations on Fasting, which will Feed you.)

Isa. 58
This is the fast that God has chosen!
To loosen the bands of wickedness,
and to undo the heavy burdens.
To let the oppress go free, and
that You break every yoke.

The 2nd

Prayer

Prayer is your desired holy (His will – Psalm 119) prayers - requests – supplications, Which should also be in tune with the Lord's.

Gospels
"Whatsoever you ask the Father in My name He shall give it to you".

The 3rd

Holy Flesh

A new Wineskin (holy - clean flesh) for new Wine (Holy Spirit). The reason I love Fasting is because it makes Me brand new every time! I always look forward to the next fast for a new body and new soul.

1 Cor. 6:19
Know you not, that your body is the Temple of the Holy Ghost?

Regular Fasting throughout the year was part of God's divine agenda for the holy flesh. For the whole nation of Israel (the Body of Christ) was under the harness of God. This was a quarterly throughout the year that was to be kept by all. God has always been in the business of perfecting the flesh of His people.

Zech. 8:9
Thus, says the Lord of Hosts,
The Fast of the 4th month and the fast of the 5th month,
and the fast of the 7th month and the fast of the 10th month,
shall be to the House of Judah joy and gladness, and cheerful feasts,
therefore, love truth and peace!

Trading food for the thick presence of the Lord. Everyone looked forward to the Feast of the Fast. Time is also sucked up in the presence of God. Contrary to popular belief, Fasting is supposed to be a Feast, not a big drag on your soul and body. The feast of the Fast is most holy with the presence of God himself.

Fasting is based on your own "Good merit system."

You are your own boss over this job of Fasting and can steer it whichever way you want by your decisions. Nobody is watching, nobody cares (but the Father), and no one is going to scold you, so you are left to trust yourself on a "good merit system" - on vitamin "No," which eventually churns out the willpower to do the will of God!

Ps. 119:109
My soul is continually in my hand, yet I have not forgotten from Your law.
(The Law of the House – "all shall be most holy")

For Christians to develop a burden to Fast, they need a blueprint for the substance of Fasting, which is in the Word, the substance of things (the Word of Fasting – meditations - Christ in You) hoped for. Fasting is the major leagues, and even a marine would have trouble getting through a Fast – never mind a Fasted life! You need the Grace of God through His word to inspire, create, and energize the power and desire to Fast. (Fasting blueprints for the substance of Fasting up ahead.)

It is one thing to be faithful and keep Your daily devotional in the Word on a loaded belly and blood, but to be faithful when You are 14 days into the Wilderness (Fasting). The weight of the Bible is heavy in Your hand, is an entirely different kind of warfare, of the highest Spiritual order because it is with the whole heart, which includes the spirit, soul, and body (Fasting – holy blood - true repentance) in the arena of suffering for His namesake.

I have spent years in these meditations and found much inspiration in them that took Me over the top. The meds invite God's participation through His word to appropriate the willpower to Fast! Fasting and meditating will flip the desires of the body and soul from the carnal to the Spiritual, training the hands for war (Fasting) and the fingers to fight (retaining the Holy Flesh for the Wisdom of God).

You cannot judge a Fast by its cover. The first 5-10 fasts will be rough, but You should not be discouraged. This will all change as the blood and belly clean up, and the toxic waste level comes down, setting you on the Path of the Ancients.

Then You will truly meditate on His word, and have respect unto His ways, and delight Yourself in the Law of the Lord. The first few Fasts are very intense and drudging (if You even make it through), and this might discourage the Faster towards the next Fast. This is because of the high volume of toxic waste being eliminated, causing a disposition of the body and soul by the minute!

This happens through every opening of the body, including the pores of your skin, the tongue, and the nose. The amount of phlegm and mucous and gas that comes out of you in just 1 Fast is shocking (You will need a spittoon by you all the time)! Your body will be unloading all this toxic waste (that has been growing all the years of your life without Fasting-cleansing) by the minute for the whole Fast.

You get more than comfortable after a few years of Fasting, with an empty body and a full Spirit instead of a full body and empty Spirit.

The Faster will eventually comprehend the value of the complete, deep, and comprehensive cleansing of the Interior of your body reaching the farthest, deepest crack and crevice of the 26 feet of compressed intestines - and of the whole body.

This understanding of the deep cleanse will also serve as an anchor for your decision-making in the Fast.

"I do not want to eat anything because it will interrupt the deep cleanse that is going on which has taken 4-5 days to get to this priceless Interior cleansing."

Not interfering with the "deep cleanse" generates much inspiration to execute all the judgments of saying "No" that are involved in just 1 Fast.

The cost of a new Wineskin is worth the Divine Design with all kinds of Living waters flowing out of a pure belly, flowing in a pure bloodstream, with the Body in fear and trembling before God Almighty and his neighbor!

GOD DOES NOT WANT JUST ANYBODY TAPPING INTO HIS POWER (Isa. 58) SO, HE RESERVES HIS POWER FOR THE POOR (of flesh and world)) AND THE NEEDY (of Him), with a tamed (Fasted) tongue!

SO DO NOT JUDGE THE POTENTIAL OF FASTING BY THE FIRST 7-10 FAST
(See Isaiah 58 for God's blessings of Fasting).

Fasting is the key to holy flesh and ushers in the blessings of God's Covenant. It is part of God's Spiritual security in His power.

You need to climb the mountain (holy flesh - fasting) with a new Wineskin to get to the top! I would imagine that Jesus brought just enough food (if any at all) to sustain the weaker Ones. By the time They got up there, their holy flesh (Fast) would have been fit for the Glory of God. I would venture to say that it was a gruesome, long trek for the Boys.

I can almost hear them saying again and again, "Are we there yet"?

NOTHING ABOUT SERVING JESUS IS EASY WHEN IT COMES TO THE FLESH.

This is Our daily burden, Our daily grief to be cherished, Our cross to bear while still here in this un-regenerated body: on this un-regenerated planet. It is no picnic cleansing the blood and the purging of the flesh and soul (carnal mind) with Fire (Fasting), for every Sacrifice will be salted with Fire (burning cleanse of the Fast), and Salt (Word): the test of Our Faith tasting much better than the finest morning coffee. My first Fast was mostly on My back, just trying to make it through, because of an unbridled eating lifestyle: filling the body with a constant food intake, on top of a constant unresolved digestive process.

The body piles up all the excess waste wherever it can (getting caked on the inside of everything) to accommodate the next "uncalled" incoming meal while still trying to digest the last meal. Recklessly filling up with the just deserts of my life, being alienated from a clean bloodstream.

("Christ in You, Your hope of glory").

Lev. 11
The Life of the flesh being in the blood!

Hot, cold flashes from the body and a lot of other undesirables, not to mention the fiery darts of the devil. I did nothing whatsoever on My first 6 Fasts except lay around and suffer!

In My early years of Fasting, I was just hanging on. Five years later and 37 escalating Fasts, I find Myself now on the 38th day of a Fast, 3 weeks past the due date of the break of the Fast, writing this section of the book with no side effects. Also tracking each Fast (see Fast Tracking Chart) and monitoring the body to compile the information for this book.

The first 5-6 Fasts were on My back (physically and spiritually). I was walking and then running in the paths of His commandments, and then I was soaring to the high places (in Christ Jesus) of the earth and Feeding on the Heritage (My Inheritance) of Jacob. All due to the low toxic waste level, clean belly and clean blood, thus, a clean interior (a holy Temple) - holy flesh - the Circumcision of Christ, in the putting off the body the sins (garbage) of the flesh.

Fasting not only cleans the blood and soul, but it disciplines the body and brings it under the control of the Holy Spirit. So, let us put our unclean blood on God's altar of humility through Fasting. God wants Us to flourish as a weeping willow tree, bowing over, pregnant with the tears of God, and driven by the Burden of Zion and his word!

Fasting is a serious Kingdom business! You need to count the cost and resolve in Your heart to the suffering for His namesake, for the glory. This is crucial: half the battle is won in the resolve alone. Resolve in Your heart to suffer for Him, and then You will reign with Him. The thorn (Fasting) is worthy of fresh Manna, which breaks every yoke!

One day, while I was Fasting, I perceived how unclean My interior was, with 30 years of surfeiting (overeating) in all kinds of foods and condiments, each meal never fully digested and eliminated before the next meal came in.

The digestive system having to leave the old meal to do the new one, leaving an ongoing back-lag of food, not eliminated, piling up exponentially into toxic waste, and all the while the body conforming to its polluted blood and comfortable in it! The life of the flesh being all spent up, manifesting itself in Spiritual deficiency, disease, and sickness.

Ecc. 4:5
The fool folds his hands and consumes (eats up) his own flesh!

Who knows what's growing in there?

It doesn't matter if you are the healthiest eating person on the planet; you are still a lifetime away from undigested food, plaguing and caking the interior walls, infecting the blood, while the body and soul get drunk on food. If you have never cleaned your house (body) before by Fasting, it is a mess, and the Holy Ghost is trying to clean it up. So, get the outer man out of the way!

It will take about 20 Fasts to clean it up and obtain a healthy body (holy flesh)! It took two years (8 Fast) of Fasting to bring down the toxic waste level in My body to 50%, and another two years (8 Fast) to 25%, with Spiritual stamina increasing each time. I AM still working on the rest! Everything that God wants to do in You needs to be through the holy (healthy) flesh, it is the Law of the House (holiness). That is why Christians today are not exhibiting the riches of Christ in their lives and in the world.

You cannot get around it; Fasting is the only way to come into the holy flesh because it's with the whole heart (blood).

You are, whatever the state of the belly is, which is the source of living waters - the core of your Salvation in Christ Jesus.

The holy flesh (clean blood and belly) is God's tap for Living waters that is automatically shut off to the unclean and automatically turned on for the holy Ones Israel (saints), who believe in the "Law of house," and even the law of the Spirit of Life in Christ Jesus!

But after a short while (of true waiting on the Lord), You will be walking around in the Fast, with intermittent Spiritual work, but meditation is still a challenge (wandering of the mind because of suffering).

It won't be long before you're on the Path of the Ancients, which leads to those fat, goodly pastures (the Word) of the Lord that drop with fatness for the soul!

The Father, in His infinite Wisdom, has provided the earth with seed for the Sower, for the fruit of the land, for the nutrition of the human body. Both the earth and man are self-sustained by God. The Father, in His infinite Wisdom, has also provided incorruptible Seed (nutrition) for the soul of man - for the New Creation, that is, the Christ in You, the hope of glory, which is sustained by the Bread and Water of Life which is the Word of His power.

This incorruptible Seed of God (the Bread of Life) needs to be sowed from the Word of God (Divine blueprint) in to your soul by the mouth (confession) into your heart just like you do with food for your body. Unlike food which is digested in hours, the Bread and Water of Life might take a week to months to be digested and felt because the Lord is doing the digesting according to His will (holiness) in your life.

Spiritual food takes longer to digest than regular food, so be patient when feeding your soul (thoughts – feelings – Words – imagination - the "will"), for the Word of God is alive and powerful, the anchor of Truth throughout all ages.

The Bread of Life is soul food.

An example of the substance (Bread of Life) of Faith.

(From "Blueprints for Meditations" - Fasting Meditation # 2 - "The Bread of Life")

Jn. 6
I AM: the Bread of Life
He who comes to Me shall never hunger (in your soul)
and he who believes on Me shall never thirst.

Rev. 10
So, I went up to the angel, and said to him, give Me the little Book.
And he said to Me, take it and eat (meditate) it up.
It will make Your belly bitter, but in Your mouth sweet as honey.

Jer. 15
Father, I found Your words and did eat them; they are unto Me a joy and rejoicing in My heart.
(And a strength, and a strengthening in My soul; and a filling, and a fulfilling in My body).

Ps. 119
Your Word is as honey to my lips.

Job 23
Oh Jesus, I have esteemed the Words of Your mouth more than My necessary food.
Feed Me with food that is convenient (Fasting) for Me,
that I be not full and deny You!

Mt. 4
Therefore, I do not live by the Word of God alone,
but by bread also. (My Holy Ghost Version.)

Pro. 12
A slothful man does not roast that which he took in the hunt,
but the substance (Bread of Life) of the Righteous is precious.

When the outward man stops eating, the Inner Man begins eating!

FASTING AND FAITH or FEASTING AND FEAR.

How do we eat the bread of Life?

Pro. 12:27
The sluggard does not roast that which he took in the hunt (the Word of Life),
But the Substance (Christ in You – Your hope of glory) of the diligent is precious.

By roasting (memorizing) it and then swallowing (meditating) it, thus becoming one with the Word – the Word made flesh. Like we did with the alphabet when we were young, we will never forget the alphabet because we are one with it, its memorized and swallowed (used). We also need the Word made flesh in Us.

One Scripture at a time, one day at a time, until the hunt is complete!

The Bread of Life takes time to digest morally and holy in your daily life.

The reality of the Kingdom (the Feast of Fasting) in You comes by the Word of Light, through meditation: as you eat the scriptures by spending time in them to allow them to become flesh in you. Substituting the Bread of Life for meals will flip the soul over to God as you fight the good fight of faith. I have provided 4 Fasting meditations up ahead that can be substituted for meals to the satisfaction of your soul while your stomach is still asleep.

In order to meditate (Spiritually feed), you need a repertoire of Scriptures to memorize, as a substantial Feed, which requires at least 15-20 Scriptures on the plate to Eat, a blueprint of the desired subject for your hope - to build up the loins of your mind. A substantial meal to produce an image of the desired Word that your inner Man (Faith) can see.

You cannot eat just a few kernels out of a seven-course (the Lord's table) meal every day and expect to have the strength to do anything!

The Lord wants His children with fat souls, for the Paths of the Lord drop with fatness (for the soul).

The word "meditate" means "to mutter."

Proverbs tells us that the power of life and death is in the tongue and that a man's belly shall be satisfied by the fruit of his lips (outer and Inner). Meditating (swallowing the Bread of Life) is a direct Spiritual feed to the Inner Man! For a man's belly (innermost being – the inner man) shall be satisfied by the fruit of his mouth, and by the increase of his lips will he be filled. For the mouth of the Wise brings forth Wisdom and his tongue talks of judgment.

To mutter (prophesy) the Word of Life with the tongue of the inner Man (Christ in You) is deeply enriching to the soul and body and uniquely profound every time!

Ps. 104
My meditation of Him will be sweet: I will be glad in the Lord.

Meditation of the Word is prophetic: You prophesy to your Spirit (inward Man), in righteousness and true holiness, the communication of Your faith firing up every good thing in You, in Christ.

As a king (queen), reigning on Your throne of judgment (the will) over Your soul and body, scattering all evil with Your eyes, as a Stranger in the earth, looking for that City (the Christ in You) whose Maker and foundations are God.

With the Word of His power being fitted for the lips as a precious jewel. Your mouth is a well of Life pouring out the mysteries of God. Your tongue as the pen of God, writing the Words of Life on the hearts of the children of men, as a true Scribe of the Lord!

He who tills (meditates) his land (heart) shall have abundant food,
but he who chases fantasies (wastes time) lacks judgment.

The tilling of the heart is the co-laboring together with the Word of His power until it is the "Word made flesh in you". In other words, until the Language of Heaven (the Word) becomes fluid in your mouth.

"For out of the abundance of the heart, the mouth speaks".

Fasting is the tilling of the body and soul, which, when coupled with the Bread of Life (the Word) makes the ultimate meditation. Fasting chastens the soul, and if you chasten yourself to bear more Fruit, then God doesn't have to, for the Fruit (growth) comes through nurture (the Word) and chastening (separation to the holy flesh). Fasting - meditation are invincible but a long-lost art in today's modern Church, and the world. Most Christians do not care to make time to meditate on the Christ in Them (the Precious) in this deadly fast-paced world with the spirit of mammon!

S.O.S 2
I sat under His shadow with great delight, and His fruit (Word) is sweet to my taste.

The difference between reading and meditating is a tasty, great delight.
To daily eat just a few Kernels of Corn out of a seven-course meal
is pointless and futile.

Ps. 119
With My lips have I declared all the judgments of Your mouth.
Meditation exceeds reading, like light exceeds darkness.
Reading is superficial, meditating is super spiritual.
Reading is natural (the exterior), meditating is divine (the Interior).

Fasting exceeds meditation because of the many sufferings (mental) for His namesake (while in the Fast) and the common good of all, which always outweighs everything! We read to learn, but we meditate to grow, we fast to forge the willpower needed to execute the will of God in Our lives as Servants of the Most-High.

So much time is wasted in a day because of doing nothing or doing the wrong thing!

Jesus wants the Christian's light breaking out as the morning, and the health of the body Divine, and trembling at His word, with the Righteousness thereof hemming him in on every side, and the glory of the Lord for inspiration.

He wants to guide Us, satisfy the soul in the dry times, and make fat the bones.

Like a watered Garden, whose waters fail not, he wants to give Us that which is Good (Christ in You).

HE WANTS TO MAKE US GREAT BY HIS GENTLENESS.

Feeding the New Creation

(Feeding the Christ in Us, the hope glory)

1 Pt. 1
Therefore, as new-born babes in Christ,
desire the sincere milk of the Word,
that you may grow by it.

Meditating (memorizing) and spending quality time with the Word is a direct Spiritual feed to the inner Man: the Christ in Us, that He may grow in Us!

Every time We meditate on the Word, We come to Jesus, knowing He will not leave Us hungry. For He satisfies Our longing soul and fills the hungry soul with goodness.

(Since the body is shut down, the suffering is just in the soul, which He fills with goodness.)

And if We thirst enough for Him, He will also give Us His spiced Wine (revelations of Him and His kingdom) to drink, even the Nectar (the Anointing) of His pomegranates. The Word wants to give you God's butter and honey (spiritual food) to eat (meditate) so that I may know how to refuse the evil and choose the good. And this will cause Us to sit under His shadow with great delight, His fruit being sweet to Our taste. The Word will feed Us with the finest of Wheat (word), and with the honey (word), out of the Rock, will the Word satisfy!

Eze. 3
Eat this book and go speak to the house of Israel. So, I opened my mouth,
and He caused me to eat (meditate) the book.

Son of man, cause your belly to eat, and fill your bowels (inward Man)
with this scroll that I give you. Then I did eat, and it was
in my mouth as honey for sweetness.

The Bread of Life is designed to be Eaten (memorized - meditated – swallowed) by confession of the mouth of the inward Man, not so much read. This holiness (separation to the Word spiritually) is imperative for holy meditation of the Word and will provide this deep feed for the inward Man.

Eating has always been better than reading!

But unlike natural food, spiritual food (Truth) takes longer to digest, for it must be weaved into the fabric of your daily life. Both by the Spiritual feed and by the test of one's Faith! It takes time for Spiritual digesting because the Lord is the one doing the digesting, It is My experience that meditation in the arena of Fasting provides the fullest, richest, and deepest feed for the inward Man: for strength in executing the many judgments involved in obeying the Lord. Therefore, it is important to establish daily feedings (meditation), rather than readings.

A repertoire of scriptures, as a smorgasbord that the Lord may serve on the table that is set before you, even in the presence of Your enemies. For the Lord himself is our portion and the cup of our inheritance.

Much like stocking your fridge, you just take it out and heat it up; but you need to work- cook (memorize – meditate) to get the food in the fridge (heart).

Once the Word is memorized (swallowed), it may be easily heated up (re-called) in about half an hour, ready to serve for the Party (Church).

Pro. 12
*But the slothful man does not roast (eat-meditate) that which he took in the hunt:
the substance of the diligent is precious.*

When eating in the natural a regular person will have 3-4 meals a day to sustain him. So is the need for inward Man (the Christ in You).

He must be fed at least 3-4 times a day, if not all day, to obtain holy flesh (through fasting – clean blood and belly) for the Holy Spirit and to make the soul and spirit fat and the body lean.

Ps.65
All the paths of the Lord drop with fatness in the Wilderness (in Him).

The Psalmist had a very fat soul and fed his hidden Man of the Heart 7 times a day.

Ps.119
Seven times a day I give You praise because of the judgments of Your righteousness.

Ps. 36
*I AM: abundantly satisfied with the fatness of Your house.
You will make me to drink from Your river of pleasures.*

P.S.

A lot of baby Christians have gone stillborn through the ages, trying to strengthen themselves in their iniquity (flesh–idolatry)!

The Great Spiritual Feed of the Great Psalm 119

"A whole heart"

Ps. 65
The paths of the Lord drop with fatness.

This Psalm alone has over:

400	Personal pronouns	My, I, Me, "I will" – (solid foundation).
150	Personal references to God's word	Understanding Him.
65	Requests	12 for the Quickening (energizing) of the Holy Ghost.
25	Vows	Breathed out of your Heart to the Father.

Ps.119
I have persuaded my heart to perform Your statues, at-all-times.

Some ones' Child could gain a lot of mileage, and cover a lot of holy ground (understanding - holy flesh) with this one Psalm!

If we prayed once a day for a week, we would have sowed (eternally invested):

2800	Personal pronouns	(My, I, Me, "I will" - (solid foundation).
1050	Personal references to God's word	Understanding Him.
485	Requests	84 for the Quickening (energizing) of the Holy Ghost.
175	Vows	Breathed out of your heart to the Father

All in 1 week!

Mt. 13
To Him who has, more shall be given,
while he who has not, from him will be taken even what he has.

WITH ALL THE MANY "I WILLS," YOU KNOW YOU WILL!

Consider the Spiritual volume of just this one Psalm if prayed once a day – 40 min. - for 10 weeks

35,000	Personal pronouns	I, Me, My, "I will" – (solid foundation)
10,500	Personal references to God's word	-understanding Him
4,850	Requests	840 for the Quickening
1,750	Vows	Breathed out of your Heart to the Father.

Imagine the harvest of this Psalm over 1 year, or like myself, over 5 years!

Pro 18
A man's belly shall be satisfied by the fruit of his mouth,
and by the increase of his lips shall he be filled;
For the power of life and death is in the tongue.

It takes a lot more willpower than you think to keep the Word, and Fasting will get You over the top! This Psalm provides the skill set to build the willpower (heart - throne) to keep His word" and to Fast.

Mt. 13
To Him who has, more shall be given, while he who has not,
from him will be taken even what he has.

To Him who has, more shall be given, while he who has not:
even what he has, shall be taken away from him,

My 9-year-old daughter has been in this Psalm for 7 years now. Started when she was 4 years old!

I weaved it into her vocabulary, covering a lot of holy ground. She is forever stuck to His testimonies.

Communion in Fasting

A person can only Fast by the Grace of God; there is no other way! Fasting is much more work than you can ever imagine. Thus, the blessings are for sure. Communion represents all God's flesh on the altar, and My participation of this Covenant by My flesh upon the altar, as a living sacrifice, bringing My body under the dominion of My throne (will) of judgment.

The Faster should start every Fast with Communion!

Communion reinforces Your commitment to the Fast by making a Covenant with God (this will close off all roads for turning around and quitting}, which locks in the Fast by the Blood Covenant of God. You see, it's a good merit system with nobody watching over You but God! You need to be honest with Yourself: this fortifies the Fear of the Lord in each battle, with its many temptations and opportunities for many victories in one Fast.

It is one thing to Fast because of an external disposition: a crack addict might go for a week without eating because of his burden for drugs or the lack of them. A depressed person might not eat because of their burden of self-pity. Or the artist invoked in a Fast because his craft has consumed him during his work.

But to Fast because of the fear of God and for the working of Righteousness is a different story altogether because you are always at liberty to eat at any time.

Therefore, the spiritual warfare is much more intense, constant, and relentless until you become more skilled with the Sword of the Lord (Word), that divides those flames of fire. Freestyle eating will lead to a momentum of lusts, which compound into the Spiritual life, quenching the Quickening of the Lord. How can the Anointing of God manifest in an unclean body? The interior needs to be clean so that the Holy Ghost may resonate in Us through holy flesh in a clean, holy bloodstream, as a river that flows, making glad the City of God!

It would be wise starting and ending each Fast with Communion, your free will offering unto the Lord, as a keeper of the Vineyard (Body of Christ), looking to eat the pure blood (full inheritance) of the Grape (Jesus).

Pro. 14
A sound heart (clean blood) is the life of the (holy) flesh.

Two major characteristics of Fasting

The 1st sign - is the stomach falling asleep.

Anywhere from 3-6 days (depending on the toxic level - sooner when the level is lower), the stomach falls asleep.

There is no more discomfort in the belly. But there still is a lifetime of food programming in mind, and smell, and the taunts of the Avenger, with his "dainty morsels". Small hairs in the belly called "cilia" are continually moving to push the food along through the digestive system. When all food is gone, these cilia fall asleep and there is no more hunger pain in the belly.

Not for about 30-50 days, depending on how unclean the interior is. (My belly is asleep within 2 days – 7 days when I first started)

But your feelings still continue to expect food at certain times, and they trigger appetite sensations in the mind, and the devil has a field day with temptations. But the Father is bigger than all that and will bring every thought captive to the satisfaction of your soul (feelings - thoughts - desires). With no more discomfort in your belly, you can now settle in and enjoy the ride (only as a seasoned Faster).

This is called a Consecrated Fast, from true hunger to true hunger (approximately 30 – 60 days), with nothing but water.

> A complete cleansing of the body and the blood, and the belly brand spanking new.
> Wait till You feel those Living waters that make your flesh tremble at His word.
> This is where the Word becomes flesh, in the holy (clean blood and belly) flesh:
> do not let it get away from You!

The 2nd sign - is the tongue.

After your stomach has fallen asleep, the tongue will have a constant filament on it (annoying)! The tongue is one of the outlets that the body uses to exit toxic waste. Burps, farting, and the pores of your skin, hair, nose, and mouth all vent the body of toxic waste. This toxic waste – old, undigested food growing at an exponential rate will lead to all kinds of deficiencies in the body, even sickness. After several years of Fasting, the toxic waste level drops tremendously.

When the belly falls asleep because there is no more food, the blood starts working on the garbage, toxic waste, cancer, or any such thing. The blood never stops working, or you will die.

The blood will keep feeding on all undesirables until there is absolutely nothing left. The blood speeds its momentum from the loss of weight and bathing the organs in the excess blood, regenerating the outer and Inner Man for the Holy Spirit, to abide forever in You.

This is the consummation of the holy flesh - the Christ in You - the Word made flesh.

The side effects of this holy blood transfusion are negative energies (only the first 7-10 days).

When Fasting, the exterior and interior are fragile. There are a lot of repercussions from shutting down the outer man. The tongue and its thorn - hot and cold flashes - equilibrium off – headaches – colon irritation – depression - rage, and a bunch of other undesirables, which is all worth living forever.

"He that does the will (Fasting) of God abides forever."

This goes on for the first couple of years, winding down as the tox-level comes down, until Your freely doing all the will of God in the Wilderness (Fasting) and delighting in it. The glory of God is not cheap. It will definitely cost you something. You do not want to be eating food when deep in a Fast, during the early years while the toxic level is high, for there is a serious kickback in the belly and in the colon that you will not like!

But as the toxic level comes down below 50%, there is then more liberty in food intake when deep into a Fast. The portion being a juice, or no more than a small handful of fruit; if you're going to anyways. Your Spiritual and physical stamina increases dramatically as the toxic level comes down, as the blood becomes clean and speeds up. This gives You liberty in emergency food intake without damage when at Your lowest state.

Your body has over 100,000 miles of blood vessels, which, if laid end to end, would stretch 2 and a half times around the Earth.

It only takes less than a minute for a drop of blood to travel from the heart, through your whole body, and back to the heart again.

The blood is cleansing the body at an incredible rate which is why I do not want to interrupt this mighty cleansing with a piece of food, interrupting this super cleanse.

"Zero ground"

(Zero Ground is a term I put together to define an empty belly and blood.)

As you Fast, your blood continues to do its job-consuming and delivering all food intake. When all the food is consumed, and there is nothing left, the blood will move on to all miscellaneous particles - drugs, toxic waste caked walls of the belly, and blood from all the undigested food to the deepest recesses of the Interior of the body, for the blood travels everywhere, scraping and cleaning whatever it can for the blood must keep working or you will die (it never stops working). When the Interior is clean, anywhere from 14-to-21 days, your blood will then move on to breaking down and eliminating anything left, including cancers, tumors, etc.

Jer. 20
For His word (the bread of Life) is in me as a burning fire shut up in my bones ...

There is a negative energy during the elimination of these undesirables, but that changes as the toxic waste level comes down (7-10 Fasts), and the Divine Design (Christ in You, the hope of glory) kicks in and starts taking over the reins. So do not judge a book (first 7 Fasts) by its cover: wait to see what's in it for you.

You can also easily monitor the belly from Zero Ground, on a clean slate, with a conscious awareness of all food intake and the bottom – mid – top of the belly, even layer upon layer when reloading the body and blood.

Ecc. 10
But the fool does not know how to get to the city of the Great King (Christ in You, the hope of glory)!

And when you get lost in the monitoring of all food intake (2-3 months), or do not know what you should eat, it's time to flip the "bitter to the sweet" and go on a Fast! It's good practise, when you lose control of your Fast, to pull back to Zero Ground. Do not throw out the baby (Fast) with the bath water. You have come too far now!

This pulling back to Zero Ground will prepare your willpower for the long major Fast, deep in the Wilderness (in Christ), that's coming for sure!

The Faster is now working out his own Salvation with fear and trembling.

God carries You for the first couple of years, but then You are Fasting on Your own in and the understanding (of the deep cleanse) thereof.

It has taken 4 years in the Fasting arena to finally finish 1 Fast correctly!

P.S.

I know who I AM:
I know where I AM going:
And I know how to get there!

Fruits and Gifts of Fasting

There are fruits and gifts of the Holy Spirit, and they are all in Christ in You, your hope of glory! And our heavenly Father would have us flowing in all of them!

These gifts and fruits should be Faster's primary target so we may enter into the fullness of Christ to love our neighbors more deeply and efficiently.

(My neighbor being anyone standing beside me.)

We need to be fully equipped to meet every need as God's ambassadors on earth!

Fruits:

Gal. 5
Love – joy – peace – patience – kindness – goodness – faithfulness
generosity – gentleness – modesty - self-control – chastity

Gifts:

1 Cor. 12
Word of Wisdom – word of knowledge – faith – healing – miracles –
prophecy – discerning of spirits – unknown tongues.

Humility

Isa. 57
Thus, says the High and Lofty One that inhabits eternity, whose name is Holy.
I dwell in a high and holy place, with Him also, that is of a contrite
and humble spirit; To quicken the spirit of the humble
and to revive the spirit of the contrite (crushed) Ones.

The lower you go, the higher you get!

Fasting will absolutely squash your pride and bring you to your most basic self. God wants the uncleanness of your soul and body crushed so the soul may thrill with joy. He does it by you, through the Circumcision of Christ – the finished work of Christ for the Child of God, In the "putting off of the body the sins of the flesh," which produces a whole heart, which includes body soul and spirit, and Fasting speeds up this process The holy Father wants His children holy, despising evil; not just trying to stay away from it. We need to eschew the evil of our soul and flesh - and God does this so gradually you think it's from yourself.

Ps. 18
Your gentleness has made me great for You have caused my mountain (Faith) to stand.

Fasting will keep the spirit of pride (world) at bay and not puffed up by the leaven of the outer man. Fasting is God's thorn of the flesh (chastening) for the growing Christian receiving revelation and knowledge from God.

Let not the foot of pride come against Us, Jesus, and let not the hand of the wicked remove.

Remove what?

Remove what? Your fearfully and wonderfully made holy flesh (a whole heart – body, soul, and spirit) where the Christ in you resides, your hope of glory (Who needs to be fed and nurtured)!

It is wise to prune – chasten (by Fasting) yourself, and then the Father does not have to!

You and God would appreciate you chastening yourself.

Jn.15
Every branch in Me that bears not fruit, He takes away, and every branch
that bears fruit He purges (chastens - humbles), that it may grow more fruit.

All the glory of Jesus came through His humility as the Son of Man, in His total submission to the Father. Humility comes through Fasting, giving Yourself as a true living sacrifice on the altar (Word) of God. Denying yourself life (food) and laying down Your life for God, and neighbor, and the common good of all, including yourself!

Fasting alone is the highest form of prayer and submission to God, for you are laying down your life with the greatest return of glory. A true labor of love for God, man, and yourself. The power of God is in the humility of Wisdom. Wisdom is the principal thing that lays hands on the sick, casts out devils, and baptizes the children of men in the Holy Ghost.

Lowliness of Mind

Ecc.7
*The heat of the Wise is in the house of mourning,
but the heart of fools is in the house of myrrh (pleasure).*

There needs to be graveness in the soul, which the holy flesh (Fasting) will maintain and retain. Fasting induces a slow mode, allowing patience to have Her perfect work. The mind slows down, thoughts slow down, the speech slows down, and everything slows down, but the clean, holy blood speeds up, carrying with it Spiritual stamina which makes an excellent atmosphere for meditating.

When you are deep in a Fast, you are in no hurry; in whatever you do.

Acts 20
Serving the Lord with all lowliness of mind and with many tears.

Low on physical stamina but high on Spiritual stamina. The Faster finds comfort at the feet of Jesus (Word), and You do not want to be too far away from Him (Word) at any time while in the Fast.

2 Cor. 12
When I am weak, I AM: strong.

The Burden of the Lord

THE BURDEN OF THE WORD (Psalm 119) + THE BURDEN OF ZION (Lamentations) = THE BURDEN OF THE LORD.

Jer. 23
Thus, says the Burden of the Lord …

The Burden of the Lord has much to say if one were able to hear. Fasting, along with Ps.119, will produce a "whole heart" (Body-blood, soul, and spirit), which opens the ears of the Learned to hear. Fasting builds up a capacity in your flesh to bear that which is lacking in the Body of Christ. Fasting provides time and space for the Burden of His word to evolve into the Burden of Zion, which will instill a deep Burden in You about the things that really matter in your life.

The Burden of the Lord is backed up by the authority of Heaven, with "Your mouth as the mouth of God."

Prophesying the heartbeat of God that is shut up deep in the bone,
being poured out as a drink (tears) offering unto the Lord that
flows down like a river, watering the land of Promise
from the womb of the Dawn.

True Repentance

Joel 2
Now, says the Lord, turn you to Me, with all your heart (whole heart – body, soul and spirit),
and with fasting, weeping, and with mourning.

True repentance requires a whole heart, which = body, soul, and spirit. We cannot leave out the body, which requires Fasting for holy blood and flesh. Most Christians lack a repentant body (Fasting). This harmonization (fulness) of body, soul, and Spirit will give You the desires of Your heart, with the Lord Himself at Your right-hand Man (Ps. 16:8).

(If You are His right-hand Man!)

Fasting works true repentance because it deals with the core of the interior, the innermost being, in a whole heart, and it works the exterior, the flesh, with the Spirit binding the two together, thus a whole heart.

The power of God for you and the Church is under the Spiritual circuit breaker of the holy flesh (Holy Spirit),
lest His power be abused.

Another Words,
the Father can trust you with His power when you are willing to suffer for His namesake's.
Fasting gives you ample opportunity to suffer for His namesake anytime, anywhere
in the arena of Fasting (humility - Wisdom), in the Harness of God.

Ps. 119.
Rivers of water run down My eyes because they do not keep Your law.

Psalms 119 is where you will find the intricate workings of a whole heart – the Circumcision of Christ - and the Burden of the Word. Fasting churns out a whole heart and clean blood, being Spiritually strong in weakness (Fasting). The Burden of the Lord will plow through the mundane life of the soul and the flesh like the 12 team oxen of Amos.

Fasting runs very deep, past the psyche, even down to the D.N.A.!

THANK YOU, FATHER, FOR THE BURDEN OF ZION AND THE BURDEN OF YOUR
WORD, EVEN THE BURDEN OF THE LORD,
SHUT UP DEEP IN MY BONES LIKE A BURNING FIRE!

Faith

Fasting and Faith are related and similar in many ways.

They are allies together in the Battle of the Ages with the same weapons (mouth and heart) of warfare! They both deal with mountains, and they both have the same likes and dislikes. They both evolve in the inmost parts of the heart, with many other similarities. And together, coupled with Wisdom (power of the Word) can certainly remove any mountain.

Jesus did not start His ministry until after a 40-day Fast, at which point He became hungry, preparing His body to bear the load of the great Work ahead of Him. This is where the strong man was bound!

This is where Jesus condemned sin in the flesh.

This is where He drank the Living Waters and did eat the Honey from the Rock: during this Fast; and a previous holy life (holy flesh). Fasting will fortify the will and give you the strength of Wisdom to execute the judgments of His word, which includes all the Goods of the Righteousness of God. Here and now, in this life! The disciples were having trouble with the Word of His power and asked Him why they could not cast out the devil, and Jesus said,

Gospel
"Howbeit, this kind only comes out by prayer and fasting."

In other words, not enough power (holy flesh - Authority). Fasting always delivers! Fasting produces a tenacity for Faith, from all the faithfulness executed in all the many temptations (win or lose), exercising discipline by just being in the Fast. You still end up with the victory of the Battle in the end, by just Fasting!

Faith, coupled with Fasting (a holy blood stream - Temple), gets the ear of God and demons. The Father always hears the cry of the Poor and Needy in Christ Jesus! Saying no all day long, holding on to the Vow that you're bringing to the House of the Lord on Sunday as a true offering, the integrity thereof lifting You up into much Faith and worship: even the high places of the earth.

Faith needs Fasting for stamina and full growth. It is the fertilizer Faith thrives in, with the will continually on call.

All the faithfulness in saying no to all the many temptations produces a Faith that is groomed by the fear of the Lord (Fasting), perfecting holiness (holy Flesh) in the fear of God.

If We walk by the Spirit, let Us also Eat by the Spirit, bringing forth fruit (Holy Flesh and Words) that is fit for repentance and the Word of Life. There is an intimate connection between a person and their food: it is a serious, major part of their life, and it takes a lot of Fasting (Faith) to break your lifetime bond with the flesh. Jesus must be Lord over this very personal area of Your life and everything else in it, or He is not Lord over all.

When was the last time you consulted the Lord about what, where, when, and how to eat and when to Fast?

Rm. 8
For I reckon that our sufferings of this present time are not worthy
to be compared to the glory that shall be revealed in Us.

FASTING - Meditation #1

Pre-meditation

Pro. 24
*I will prepare My work without (Fasting - the flesh), and make it fit for the field (My heart):
then afterwards, I will build My palace (the Christ in Me).*

Pro. 14
A Wise woman builds her mansion: but the foolish plucks it down with their hands.

Theme

Ecc. 6:7

All the labor of man is for his mouth, yet his appetite is not filled.

Ps. 73:

They set their mouth against the heavens and their tongues walk through the earth.

Pro. 18:

*A man's belly (spirit) shall be satisfied by the fruit of his mouth
and by the increase of his lips shall he be filled,
for death and Life are in the power of the tongue:
and they that love it (Life in Christ Jesus) shall eat the fruit (Life) of it.*

Introduction

Ecc. 10:16-17

*Woe to you, O land (heart),when your king (will) is a child,
and your princes look to eat in the morning.*

*But blessed are You, O land (Heart),
when Your king (will) is the son of nobles (trained by experience),
and Your princes eat in due season, for strength and not for gluttoness.*

Pro. 30:8

*Jesus is curbing My desires to feed Me with food that is convenient for Me,
lest I be full and deny Him.*

Content

Pro. 23:1-3

*When you sit down to eat with a ruler, consider carefully what is before you:
and put a Knife (Word of God) to your throat, If you are a man given to appetite.
Be not desirous of his dainties: for they are a deceptive meat.*

For they that are such, serve not our Lord Jesus Christ, but their own belly:

Ps. 26:10

"Watch for the food bribes".

1 Cor. 6:13

Meats for the belly, and the belly for meat, but God shall destroy them both.

Pro. 23:6-8

Eat not the bread of him that has an evil eye, neither desire his dainty meats:
For as he thinks in his heart, so he is: "Eat and drink",
he says to you, but his heart is not with you.

The morsel which you have eaten you will vomit up, and lose your sweet (anointed) Word.

Phil. 3:19

Whose end is their destruction and whose god their belly.

Pro.29:4

Therefore I, as king (over My soul and body), establish My land (Christ in Me)
by judgment (right decisions), but to receive bribes destroys it.

Isa. 55:1-2

Everyone that thirsts,
you come to the Waters: and he that has no money, you come, buy and Eat;
yes, come buy Wine and Milk (the Spirit and Word of God) without price!
Why do you spend money on that which is not Bread?
and Your labor for that which satisfies not.

Hearken diligently unto Me, Eat that which is Good (Bread of Life),
and let your soul delight itself in fatness.

Ps.23

You prepare Table (the Word) before Me in the presence of mine enemies.

Pro. 15:17

Better a dinner of herbs (the Spirit) where love is,
than a sumptuous steak (flesh) and the hatred therewith.

Ps. 36:8

I AM: abundantly satisfied with the fatness of Your house.
You shall make Me to drink from Your river of pleasures.

78:23-25

He commanded the clouds from above, and opened the doors of heaven
and rained down Manna upon Them, and did give Them the
Corn of Heaven, and man did eat angel's food.

Lk. 1:53

He has filled the Poor (in flesh) with good things,
but the rich (in the flesh) He has sent away empty handed.

Ps. 16

The Lord is My portion and the cup of My inheritance.

Summary

Ps.119:14

How sweet are Your words unto My taste! Yes, sweeter than honey to My lips.

Pro, 24:13-

I do eat Honey because it is good and the Honeycomb, which is sweet to My taste,
so is the knowledge of Wisdom to My soul.
When I find it, there is a reward, and My expectation will not be cut off.

Pro. 27

The full soul despises the Honeycomb: but to the hungry soul every bitter thing is sweet.

Ps. 128:1-2

I AM: blessed because I fear the Lord; I walk in His ways.
I will eat the labor of My hands (faith).

I will be happy: it is well with Me!

Pro 20

Food won by fraud taste sweet, but later the mouth will be filled with gravel!

Chapter 7

"In the Fast"

Ps. 72
*Truly God is good to Israel, to such that are of a
pure (whole) heart (including clean blood - Fasting).*

Fasting brings about a complete, natural blood transfusion, in its own Divine design from God: for we are all fearfully and wonderfully made in His likeness and image. You cannot think of the heart without thinking about the blood. The whole heart implies the whole person (body, soul, and spirit - blood). For the most part, when God talks about the heart, He is talking about the blood, the life force of the heart.

"The life of the flesh is in the blood," which should flow through holy flesh.

Like the mind, the heart also has a vast, uncharted territory. The average Christian only uses a small percentage of a whole heart because of the lack of holy flesh and blood, which will only reveal a small percentage of God's light in any given circumstance, for the spirit (life force, heart-blood) of a man is the lamp of the Lord.

The 100% potential of the mind is the same as the 100% potential of a whole heart because it is backed up by God Almighty! The Father always hears and answers the cry of the Poor (of this world and the flesh) and Needy (of Jesus).

Imagine what "Whomsoever will" could do with 100% of a whole heart.

A whole heart is complicated, including the spirit, soul, and body, as one harmonized Unit. It is intricate, and extremely hard and lengthy to sort out outside of Christ (the Word). Psalm 119 will save you many years of trial and error in the pursuit of a whole heart as a Stranger on the earth!

To ignore and stay away from Psalm 119 is to deny all interests in a whole heart and its eternal potential riches! Consider clean blood (for the Spirit of Life) and holy flesh (for the Word and the Quickening) ushering in all the physical and Spiritual blessings of the Covenants of God! In due time, let Patience (Fasting) do her perfect work.

Jer.11
I will not let the holy flesh (a whole heart) pass from me.

THE HOLY FLESH IS YOUR BLANK CHECK FROM GOD TO WITHDRAW YOUR SPIRITUAL INHERITANCE FROM YOUR HEAVENLY ACCOUNT AT ANY TIME.

The Holy Flesh – Circumcision of Christ, which comes through Faith in the Word and your holy blood from Fasting, is the Harness of God, lest You stray away!

This phase of the Fast requires much meditation and willpower. The enemy will try to get you constantly meditating on the natural (food - problems), so just relax by turning your mind immediately to the Spiritual food of the Word.

It will satisfy You.

Fill up on the Honey from the Rock ("Blueprints for Meditation" – Fasting #1-2-3-4). This will smooth out the very bumpy ride in your head (not your belly). As you mature in Fasting (as the toxic waste level comes down), in years to come You will have a lot more physical and Spiritual stamina with quietness from food temptations. I just came off a 36-day Fast with quietness, not much food temptation, and comfortable in it! Yes, My belly, tongue, and mind are comfortable in Christ, like the weaned Child of God that I AM.

Lay the foundation (holy flesh) for the glory of the Spirit of God. The Holy Spirit wants to get to the outside, on holy flesh, so that He may be contagious to others!

Go for it!

Fasting is no picnic for the outward man (in the beginning) but a vacation and feast for the Inner Man (as the toxic level comes down). It is going to take a lot of resistance to stay in the Fast, and resolving in the heart to suffer, will ease the stress. Fasting brings the War to your door!

COUNT THE COST AND THE GLORY!

You are fearfully and wonderfully made. Adam was clothed with Light in the Image of God. He did not even have to eat. And today, the true Christian has the light of the glory of God in the face of Christ, in him. (On the inside, let's get it to the outside.) You do not have to worry while Fasting, and You are safe in the Divine Design of the Lord!

Just leave the body alone - relax - hang on - and enjoy the Ride!

WITH EVERYTHING SHUT DOWN, YOU WILL HAVE PLENTY OF TIME FOR MEDITATION AND THE FEEDING OF THE SOUL.

The soul needs to eat as well as the body. You are aiming for a very fat soul. Eating one of these meditations will quiet the mind in about 40 minutes, but once memorized (swallowed – like the Alphabet), they will soar You into the high places (Divine revelations of God) of the earth (not to the low places of the flesh - pride and food), quenching all those sizzling, dainty morsels of the devil.

Undigested food will dilute and pollute the Way of your physical and Spiritual life.

The stomach is now asleep (after 3 days), no hunger pains anymore, and the Battle of the mind has now begun. You have resolved to suffer for His namesake, with Your eyes on the Prize (Fruits and Gifts of the Spirit), and the Christ in You - Your hope of glory, and the Burden of Zion and of His word, all shut up in Your bones like a consuming fire! Fasting is not only a bunch of suffering (which is Your reasonable worship), but also an opportunity to peak into the Mysteries of God and man. So, get comfortable in it, for this is the Wilderness journey and the Harness (chastening - pruning) of the Lord.

God still takes His people through the Wilderness today and will continue to do so until He comes back and the Land of Promise is established on the earth, forever with the Father (Himself there)!

So, put on the Harness (Fasting) of God, and lock (a quality resolve) yourself in!

The Amateur Faster

My Fasting Testimony!

I was fascinated by the lifestyles of Christian heroes as a young Christian in the 1990's. I was amazed by their mighty works by Fasting and prayer. It was revealed to me by the Holy Ghost that it was because of Fasting (a whole heart – clean blood). However, as an Italian, I really enjoyed my food and put the Fasting aside. I was infatuated with the idea of Fasting and power but did not really believe I could Fast. The Devil had me convinced it was out of my reach, so I put it aside for a season (which took 10 years to come back). During those ten years, the Lord gave me a little prayer that went like this:

*"Thank you, Father for this food. I pray that You will bless
this food holy for my body for its Divine design, and
lead me into a life of Fasting, in Jesus name".*

This prayer had become my substitute for Fasting to ease my consciousness and fuel my hope for Fasting. It was a lot easier than Fasting. It made me feel better for not Fasting as the Lord wanted. But God heard and kept that confession all through all those years which eventually manifested in the natural. The Divine providence of God eventually led me into Fasting by the confession of my own mouth. So, I started Fasting in the year 2010. In my first Fast I did nothing except lay on the couch. It took my belly a whole week to fall asleep (2 days now). I was in discomfort for the whole week with temperature flashes, stomach cramps, weakness, and equilibrium off; all this because of a high toxic waste level from thirty years of accumulating undigested food.

Now, forty-five Fasts later, my belly is asleep in a day and a half, with little cramps and discomfort. Exercising, house duties, cooking for the family, and my Spiritual and physical responsibilities are all done in a day of Fasting. My toxic waste level has gone down from 100% to 20%, with a clean belly and bloodstream, fueling many physical and Spiritual blessings in my Life.

Ps. 17
They have closed-up their fat hearts; with their mouth they speak proudly.

Ps. 119
Their heart is as fat as grease; but I delight in Your law (law of the House – most holy).

The idea is the separation between the holy flesh and the natural (the carnal mind and the world).

THAT THE BLOOD BE CLEAN AND HOLY, AND THEN MAINTAINED (4 Fasts per year).

Consider cold cooking grease on the hands doing dishes. I would try to avoid the grease from getting on the hands and the other dishes because of the stickiness of the grease. It is annoying and hard to wash off.

The holy flesh and the world (spirit of Mammon) do not mix.

Indeed, it is better to be washed in the Blood of Jesus, and stuck to His testimonies!

I do a major Fast 4 times a year and small ones in between to maintain the holy flesh and blood.

When the blood and flesh get too far away from zero ground (the break of the Fast), I head back to the Wilderness Fasting). David and the John the Baptist did many times. Jesus is the fullness of the holy flesh expressed: God manifests in the Flesh and seen! His miracles came out of holy flesh and the Holy Blood of God!

Jn. 1
The Word became flesh and dwelt among us;
and we beheld His glory as the only begotten Son of God.

The Seasoned Faster

God gets excited (and so should you) when a Person humbles (crushes) the outer man for the sake of the Inner Man, laying down Your life, taking up the Cross, and following Jesus into the holy flesh, the glory of God.

Fasted life = clean belly = Clean blood = Holy Flesh = Divine perspective of the burden of the Lord.

By a Fasted life, I mean four major Fasts a year (a quarterly maintenance) for the Temple of the Lord. Including the small ones in between, as the Good Shepherd leads. I AM: always Fasting something: if not My belly, then My tongue (words), on My down time when eating again. The Fasting of the tongue (Words) is a much greater challenge because the power of life and death is in it.

A totally Fasted life: a holy eating lifestyle maintaining the upkeep of the Interior, a new fresh Wineskin for the New Wine (Holy Ghost)!

My spirit seems to be more conducive to the Kingdom of Heaven at zero ground (belly asleep), than anywhere else.

All the great Ancients of the Lord have come up through the ranks of Fasting!

It takes a mighty Man or Woman of God to Fast because of the great free-will offering of the body and the mental suffering of His namesake. Your taking up your cross, and denying yourself, and following the holy flesh (Jesus) into the Wilderness (Fasting). It is hard to finish a major Fast without piecing (a handful of food at high-stress points), but I would consider Myself a seasoned Faster (over 40 Fasts in 10 years). I have earned it in the Wilderness (the arena of Fasting), training My hands for War and My fingers to fight - carrying the Harness of God - humbling Myself under the mighty hand of God.

It takes a lot of experience (a strong will) to get through the Wilderness (Fasting) totally clean (without piecing).
But I know it can be done! It is right on the tip of My tongue!

TOAL CLEANSING = HOLY FLESH AND FAITH = TOTAL BLESSINGS AND THE QUICKENING ON CALL.

I have gone from dying on the couch (first few Fasts) to walking in the Fast to running.
In the Fast, to soaring the high places of the earth (My inheritance through meditation),
in only five years of Fasting, which is not long in the scope of Eternity.

As one becomes more mature in Fasting, food temptations become scarce: much more,
distant and weaker (but other temptations are periodic but much less intense).

There was this one time in a major Fast (14 days) when I got a hernia from yelling in a rage, then sprained my back the next day, then had a serious fight with my family, and still finished the other half of the Fast. After a while of Fasting and meditation, you start to see, feel, and appreciate the glory of the "hidden Man of the heart" as a Pearl of great price and His need to be Fed.

Your Faith will evolve into a mountain that cannot be moved: unshakeable! Fasting will catapult You into a slow upward ascent into the Authority of God by the humility (holy flesh) that comes through Fasting - the Word made flesh!

When Fasting, your Divine Design stimulates driving willpower to get the Job done. This is the desire of the Inward Man to reach the Father. He loves it! The Spiritual food starts kicking in when the outward man stops eating.

There is no growth of glory in the Church today because there is no Fasting - holy flesh that does true justice to the glory of God and the inner Man – the Christ in You, that the world may believe that the Father has sent Us.

Isa. 52
Awake, Awake; put on Your strength oh Zion (the Body of Christ; put on Your beautiful Garments, oh Jerusalem (biological Jews), the holy city, for there shall no longer come into You the uncircumcised and the unclean.

Shake Yourself from the dust arise and sit down, oh Jerusalem.
Loose Yourself from the bands of Your neck (the flesh), oh captive Daughter of Zion.

When in a Fast, Spiritual Reality is always staring you in the face,
from the Mirror of His word,
on a constant frequency, rightly dividing the Word of Truth,

AS IT PERTAINS TO THE DISPOSITION OF THE OUTER MAN TO THE INNER MAN.
TO FIX WHAT NEEDS TO BE FIXED, EVEN TO BE "AS JESUS IS."

The Interior

Deciding to eat healthy without Fasting is like sweeping dirt under your carpet. The house looks clean, but it is still there.

It does not matter if you are the healthiest person around, you still have a life-time of undigested meals and undesirables dwelling in your body.

Most people treat their bodies this way without even realizing it. There needs to be a genuine relationship with you and your body. Fasting has brought me into a relationship with My body for the first time in My life. I always know where I AM from Zero Ground (the Break of the Fast - holy flesh), and when I do not, it is time to get back to the Wilderness (Fast) because I am lost! It is easy to monitor food intake and its digestive resolve from Zero Ground (watery stool). You will be able to see the danger of surfeiting (overeating) at a distance.

Pro. 22
A wise man sees evil coming and hides himself (in the Word and Fasting).

Let's face it: the Church and every person on this planet needs to understand Themselves from the inside out. Before a person can even begin to eat Properly, they need to Fast (clean house) to get every crack and corner cleaned up through the spirit of burning (Fasting), which infiltrates the darkest recesses of the Interior.

Once the house is clean, you may start filling it again with every kind of Fruit and Charm, both New and old.

Fasting is Taming the tongue and belly day by day – hour by hour – and minute by minute! (wow)!

Pro. 18
The power of Life and death being in the Tamed (wholesome) tongue!

Remember:
All the other lusts stem from the food lust. From the very beginning, Satan came with food for the destruction of Man.

Pro. 24
So, consider diligently when you sit down to eat with a Ruler (you, ruling over the Lord with your food), and put a Knife (the Word) to your throat (speak it) if you are given to gluttony.

Piecing

Piecing is drinking or eating anything besides water before the "Break" (interrupting the total deep cleansing).

Piecing puts the digestive system and the blood on hold instead of doing their work of Renovating the Temple of the Lord.

Piecing (a handful of food) sets you back about 12 hrs. before you get back to Zero Ground (Empty Interior). And a handful of meat will take you about 20 hours before getting back to Zero Ground. This is not a good practise because any weakness in the "Break" will taint the integrity of the break of a future long Fast. This could be critical if an amateur Faster somehow got to the end of a long Fast (highly unlikely). When it comes to Fasting, "to be faithful in little is to be faithful in much" is crucial!

If you are going to a Piece some food, make it only 4 oz of juice or 1 handful of fruit.

The Lord will not allow any serious damage when Fasting. You do not have to worry about it.

I've been scared of Fasting at times, watching the outer man pine away to nothing!

Experienced a lot of discomfort physically and emotionally because of Piecing, but not really hurt. Just leave the body to its Divine Design; it knows what it is doing.

Ps. 91
No evil shall befall you, nor shall any plague come you're dwelling for the Lord has given His angels charge over You to keep You in all Your ways.

IT IS NOT WISE TO PIECE IN THE EARLY YEARS OF FASTING BECAUSE OF THE HIGH TOXIC WASTE LEVEL: YOU WILL EXPERIENCE A LOT OF DISCOMFORT FROM PIECING. JUST NOT WORTH THE SMALL RELIEF OF FOOD.

Later, as the toxic level comes down below 50%, you will have a lot more liberty in Piecing.

I can eat a small cheeseburger with no discomfort in a short 7-day Fast – but not a long Fast. I would not even consider Piecing some food in the early high-tox days! There is also a psychological disposition in piecing that sets you back physically and Spiritually because of the guilt of breaking the Vow of Fasting to your God.

You have disturbed the sleeping bear (the cilia hairs in the belly), and you do not want to wake up a sleeping bear!

The tongue is one of the ways of monitoring Your food intake when in the Fast. The tongue is very tamed and sensitive when the body is empty, so do not shock it with rich or spicy food when Piecing (even speaking is a chore in the early Fast.) Taste buds do not last for long on a Fast, and if You still feel the food on Your tongue after 10-15 minutes, there is too much food intake! Pull back missing 2-3 meals depending on the size of the Piecing, and dilute with water!

Piecing is Satan's little foxes that spoil the Vine (the Fast).

If you are going to Piece some food and you have to have something, make it a juice or small fruit.

You do not want to wake up your belly. Always remember, You do not want to wake up the sleeping bear!

A SMALL HANDFUL OF FRUIT WILL TAKE ABOUT 8 HRS TO RESOLVE (getting back to Zero Ground)

Just for a Piece! It's not worth the backtrack of 8 hrs.

There is some kick back, and it will cost you some discomfort; just not worth it. No more than a small hand full (preferably fruit- grapes), to relieve the mental and emotional stress. For the most part, Piecing is due to the stress of the soul, not the stomach (hunger does not return for weeks); it's the stress from always saying "no" – building awesome Faith (for the stomach is asleep)!

Keep the Piecing wholesome, for there is a tendency from stress to appease the flesh with the dainty morsels of the Devil and the dainty morsels of your old life. This will also affect the integrity of the future long Fast, which is coming if the Lord has His way! Do not be discouraged when Piecing; just chalk it up to maturity (Your Spiritual account and the holy flesh), for there is nothing wasted in the Lord (Fast); there are always baskets of Bread left over.

The inner Man is growing by the minute, and all things are working together for good to Them that Fast.

Pro. 13
He who keeps his mouth (food) and his tongue (Words) preserves his life.

FOOD + THE FLESH + THE WORLD = THE SPIRIT OF MAMMON

Body Venting

Any kind of working machine requires venting of some kind, and so does the human body. The body needs more ventilation than any other machine!

The body's responsive digestive clock gets buried when eating more than you should (surfeiting), along with Your food compass (location from Zero Ground), and the body venting of the potent gases (burps – farts) come down to a bare minimum, because of all the congestion (sludge) of all the undigested leftovers of meals, which compounds exponentially over the years.

THIS IS NOT GOOD FOR THE BODY.

The build-up of this toxic gas from toxic waste (a lifetime of leftover undigested meals) can be detrimental to your body. This is another reason for Fasting, to vent out all toxic gas and waste. You will be able to see from the Break of the Fast that there is an immediate response of venting (burps, farts, flehm) from those foods being taken in and processed. A clean Interior brings an immediate venting of gases with the intake of any amount of anything (high efficiency). This serious suppression of gases and waste, coupled with unclean blood, evolves into physical and spiritual shipwreck, sickness, and disease.

BUT MANIFESTING THE HOLY GHOST THROUGH YOUR HOLY BLOOD IS TRUE FAITH, INDEED.

Fasting will bring You into a working, loving relationship with Your body's interior, which You cannot see.

Fasting is the spotlight of God's word on the inner Man.

We need to understand true and false hunger and our belly's digestive timetable, which only comes from Fasting!

We need to be always conscious of where we are from Zero Ground, to retain the Holy Flesh and Wisdom, so that we can properly monitor the blood through the harness of God (a Fasted- holy eating lifestyle) consecrating both belly (food) and tongue (Words) to God: which is Our Spiritual and reasonable service of worship unto the Lord.

Ps. 119
I will praise You O Lord with my whole (body, soul, and spirit - blood) heart.

Be sure to vent out the physical stress by exercise and the Spiritual stress by the Word (meditation)! Food will not work! It makes it worse because of the stain of guilt! No water for the first 2 days will get you to Zero Ground ("the zone – empty interior") much faster, but it is much harder. A person may go a long time (30 – 40 days) without food but only 3 days without water. It is not easy to drink 6 glasses of water every day and then maintain that schedule daily, with the meals –t hen room for the Holy Ghost, in the midst of all those "conspiracy of interruptions" in one day!

A lot of practise and willpower will be needed to maintain a sufficient water intake to support the Divine Design. Water and exercise play a vital role during the Fast in the total natural transfusion of blood. The blood needs lots of water.

There is a lot of stress built up in the Fast that kicks back to the spirit in a negative energy. Meditation helps to relieve stress on the body and soul, which is the major resistance of the outer man. Any attempt for relief outside the Word of God will result in failure.

Ps. 119
This is my comfort in my affliction; Your word has quickened me.

This venting of the body is like clockwork (if the Interior is clean) and is important in monitoring. food intake, and if it is not consistently there, you have strayed from Zero Ground. The body, like any other functioning system, needs to be vented. Stress (friction) of the body and soul manifests itself in all kinds of ways. I remember coughing up flehm with black spots in it for about 6 months (on and off the Fasting), and I was worried about it at first until the Holy Ghost showed Me it was just the body cleansing itself, as the holy flesh takes over. This kind of body and blood cleansing comes only from Fasting (the Divine Design).

The Spirit of burning (Fasting) is as thorough a cleaning as you can get, reaching the innermost parts of the innermost being. So, this is what to expect: it's all part of the cleansing and humbling Package of Fasting, that the Father may exalt You "in due time."

The Long Consecrated Fast

(30-50 days – until true hunger returns)

A Consecrated Fast is from day 1, to the return of true hunger in belly – (appx. 30 to 50 days).
The physical goal of a major Fast is a new-born baby's belly and a whole heart,
with living Waters flowing in a river of clean blood, quickening
the flesh to do the will of God, all the time.

The goal of a long Fast is the New Wineskin – holy flesh – a new Temple (of God).

You hear people say, "I'm starving," all the time. Well, they are lying all the time. The average person is filled with so much fat that it would take at least a month before burning off all fat and starving. There are all kinds of testimonies of people going up to 70 days before true hunger returns to the belly. Long Fasts have been done by many – many times over –by all kinds of people.

Fasting was a common practise in religious circles of all kinds. All the prophets and ancients of old came up through the ranks of Fasting. Fasting promotes its own lifetime commitment to the Temple of the Lord because of the value of its own total deep cleansing. It will not be long before You make a life time commitment to the maintenance of Your Body (God's peculiar treasure) as you come to a place of understanding how fearfully and wonderfully We are made.

Fasting brings a serious, consistent consciousness of all the Divine inner workings inside you which also inspires and locks in the Faster to a lifetime commitment. The problem is getting through enough Fasts (10 or so) to appreciate the Divine natural blood transfusion of the Fast.

I do 4 major Fast 4 a year, every 3 months, with small ones when needed because of over-eating.

Fasting will add years to your life. Who doesn't want to live longer?

The body and mind get used to the idea of Fasting through the experiences of Fasting. The belly is asleep (no worries) and the blood is sped up – the body is enjoying its deep cleansing - all is safe and sound. The fight is mental, not so much physical. Basically, you are just waiting longer to eat.

The long Fast is safe when coupled with understanding and Faith but can be detrimental when coupled with fear.

Fasting with fear instead of Fasting with Faith is dangerous because the Fast will amplify the state the mind of the Faster. But the Bread of Life, which is the Word of His power, will amplify the mind of Christ in You, which will keep You safe.

It is very important to maintain the integrity (saying "No") of small Fasts, for they will surely lead to bigger ones as You start understanding the value of the deep cleansing and the Spiritual fruits and gifts in the Christ in You, the hope of glory.

The integrity (willpower) of the holy flesh must be maintained to prepare for a major Fast.

This integrity is crucial!

The integrity of your will is being translated (by the Spirit of Burning) into the will of God, and then into the Burden of the Word, and then into the Burden of Zion (the Church). A lot of resistance is needed because there has been a lot of discomfort going on, and justification (reasons for comfort) for the mental suffering is always lurking at the door.

FASTING - Meditation # - The Spirit of Burning!

Theme

Heb. 1:7

He makes His ministers a flame of fire.

Isa.4:4-5

The Lord will wash away the filth of the Daughters of Zion (the Church),
and purge the bloodshed (guilt) of Jerusalem from the midst thereof,
by the SPIRIT OF JUDGMENT and by the SPIRIT OF BURNING.

Rev. 9:17

Then I saw horses in a vision, and Them that sat upon them,
having breastplates of fire.

Ps.69: 9

The zeal of Your house has consumed Me.

Introduction

Jn.15:2

Every Branch in Me that bears no fruit He takes away,
and every branch that bears fruit He purges,
that it may grow more fruit.

Isa. 1:25

I will turn My hand upon you and purely purge your dross
and take away all your tin.

1 Cor. 9:26-27

Therefore, I run in such a way, as not without aim;
I box in a way, as not beating the air;

but I discipline My body and make it My slave,
so that after I have preached to others,
I Myself (the Apostle Paul) will not be disqualified.

Content

Rm. 12:1

I beseech Myself, therefore, by the Word of God,
and offer My body as a living sacrifice:
My reasonable, spiritual worship.

Ps. 69:10

I will chasten My soul with Fasting, which is to My reproach,
My burning. (So, God does not have to.)

Deut. 16:3

Father, I receive the "bread of affliction".

Lev. 3:14-16

I will bring My offering, even an offering made by fire (Fasting)
unto the Lord. (for all the fat is the Lord's!)

Mk. 9:49

My sacrifice will be salted with fire (Fasting), and salt (blessing)!

Isa. 43:2

Therefore, when I go through the fire I will not be burned:
neither will I smell like smoke.

1Pt. 1:7

That the trying of My faith, being much more precious than gold
which perishes, though it be tried by fire, is salted unto My glory.

Mt. 11:12

For the Kingdom of God suffers violence (Fasting), and the violent take it by force.

Ps. 130:1

Oh, Jesus! Out of the depths have I cried unto You.

Part b

Jn. 3:16

Therefore, the love of God in Me, is laying down My life down (Fasting)
for the Body of Christ, My family, and a lost world!

Ps. 22:26

In My affliction (Fasting), I will Eat (Honey from the rock) and be satisfied;
I will seek and praise the Lord, I will let My heart live forever.

Mt. 20:28

For I have not come to be served, but to serve and to give My life as a ransom for many.

Col. 1:24

Therefore, I now rejoice in My sufferings for You, and fill up that
which is behind in the afflictions of Christ in My flesh,
for His Body's sake, which is the Church!

Phil. 2:17niv

Even if I AM: being poured out as a drink offering on the
sacrifice and service of Your faith, I joy and rejoice with you all.

2 Cor. 12:15

I will gladly spend and be spent for the Church, though the
more abundantly I love Her, the less I be loved.

1 Cor. 8:18

For I reckon that My sufferings of this present time are not worthy
to be compared to the glory that shall be revealed in Us.

Ps.66:13

I will come into Your house with burnt offerings. I will pay My vows unto You.

Ps. 69:9

For the zeal of Your house has consumed Me!

2 Cor. 4:10

I AM: always bearing about in My body the dying of My Lord Jesus,
that the life of Jesus may also be made manifest.

Pro. 10:12

Love covers all sin! The love of God in Me never fails!
I commend Myself to every man's conscious.

Summary

Rm. 8:3

Jesus also for sin, condemned sin in His flesh, that I might know
the power of His resurrection, and the fellowship of His sufferings.

Zech. 8: 19

Thus, says the Lord of Hosts,
The Fast of the 4th month and the fast of the 5th month,
and the fast of the 7th month and the fast of the 10th month,
shall be to the House of Judah joy and gladness, and cheerful feasts,
therefore, love truth and peace (Trading food for the thick presence of the Lord.
Everyone looked forward to the Feast of the Fast).

Ps. 50:5

Gather together My saints unto Me, who have made a covenant with Me by sacrifice (Fasting)!

P.S.

Ecc. 4:5

The fool folds his hands (faith) and eats his own flesh.

The Lord's Spiritual venting for the Body of Christ the Church

The Cry — Meditation #4

("Blueprints for Meditation")

Ps. 29
The voice of the Lord is upon the waters.

(Waters - the soul – will power - feelings and emotions – tears)

Upon all the tears of the Saints, and upon the tears of the Poor (of this world) and Needy (of Jesus).

Ps. 29
The Voice of the Lord peals across the waters.

Able to save anyone, even unto the ends of the earth!

Ps. 29
The God of glory thunders upon the many, mighty waters.
There is nothing impossible for a Man or Woman of God with a whole heart.
Whose tears are the truest, purest, expression of love, in the earth and backed up by the power of God Almighty!

Ps. 119
Rivers of water run down my eyes because they keep not Your law (holiness).
Every tear is counted, stored, and noted, along with every sleepless night!

Ps. 56
You tell of My wanderings; You put My tears into Your wineskin:
are they not written in Your Book?

Ps. 29
The Lord sits as King upon the flood, forever.

The Cry – Meditation #3

("Blueprints For Meditation")

Ps. 46

There's a River whose streams (tears) make glad the City of God,
even the holy dwelling Places of the Most High.

S.O.S. 4

A garden enclosed is My sister, My spouse: a spring shut up, and a fountain sealed.

Jer. 9

Oh, that My head were waters and mine eyes a fountain of tears that I might weep
day and night for the slain of the Daughter of My people (Body of Christ).

S.O.S. 4

I AM:
fountain of gardens, a well of Living waters with streams of Lebanon.

Gal. 4

We have not received the spirit of this world, but the Spirit of adoption,
whereby we cry, Daddy God.

The Burden of the Lord is part of Our inheritance in Christ,
We are joined to Him in one Spirit: therefore,
as He is, so are We in this world

Water

Experts advise drinking 6-8 glasses of water every day for oxygen to flow freely in your body and help the kidneys and colon eliminate waste. What's best, it helps in flushing out excess sugar from your body.

Here are just a few important ways water works in your body:

Regulates body temperature.
Moistens tissues in the eyes, nose and mouth.
Protects body organs and tissues.
Carries nutrients and oxygen to cells.
Lubricates joints.
Promotes weight Loss.
Flushes out toxins.
Improves skin complexion.
Maintains regularity.
Carrying nutrients and oxygen to your cells.

Flushing bacteria from your bladder.
Critical for digestion.
Prevents constipation.
Keeps blood pressure normal.
Stabilizes the heartbeat.
Cushions the joints.
Protects organs and tissues.
Maintains electrolyte (sodium) balance.

Lessens the burden on the kidneys and liver by flushing out (Fasting) waste products. Water increases energy and relieves fatigue. And since your brain is mostly water, drinking it helps you think, focus and concentrate better and be more alert. Giving your body enough fluids to carry out all those tasks means you are staying hydrated. Some warning signs of dehydration are weakness, headaches, low blood pressure, dizziness, confusion, and dark urine.

SOME DAYS I DRINK MORE WATER THAN THE FOOD I EAT.

Water is symbolic of the Holy Spirit, the Life Giver. He sits as King upon the flood of your pure bloodstream and holy flesh. A Spiritual climate fit for the Kingdom of God is created in an empty body, with only the Bread of Life, water, and clean blood. This bedrock of holiness opens up fountains of Living waters, pouring out tears of comfort for the virgin (separated to the Word – clean interior) Daughter of Zion (Body of Christ), making glad the City of God, preferring one another in labors of love.

Pro. 18
The words My mouth are as deep waters, and the wellspring of Wisdom as a flowing brook.

Fasting wipes the steam (the world the flesh, and the carnal mind) off the Mirror of His word so that You can have a clear look at the inward Man. And once again, the inward Man does the most of His growing in Fasting, when all the natural food is gone, and the Way is clear of all obstacles, both physical and Spiritual.

We hear the term "drink lots of water", but few people realize the importance of water both physically and spiritually. Much water (and less food) is essential for a high performance of the blood, which equals a high performance of the body, soul, and spirit, which equals a whole heart (holy flesh)!

Remember:

The life of the holy flesh is in the blood, and water is critical for the blood, both physically and Spiritually. Drinking "lots of water" is critical for the full operation of the Divine Design.

This is true repentance with all your heart, and with Fasting, weeping, and mourning: For God has sent forth the Spirit of His Son into our heart to serve Him and our neighbor, with all lowliness of mind, and with many tears! God wants our tears (living Waters) for the Body of Christ to run down like a river day and night, to make glad the City of God (including Yourself)!

S.O.S. 4
A Garden enclosed is My sister, My spouse. A spring shut up, and a fountain sealed. A fountain of gardens, a well of Living waters.

Jesus, in the days of His flesh, offered up prayers and supplications with strong crying and tears. We should also labor (cry) according to His working (tears), which works mightily in "whomsoever will". Our souls should be longing, even Fasting for the courts of the Lord, The heart and flesh crying out for the living God.

Ps. 119
Oh Jesus, the zeal of Your house has consumed Me.

Fasting will get us to a place where we can cry out in the night and pour out our hearts like water before the face of the Lord for the lives of the young children who faint from hunger (Bread of Life) at the top of every street!

Pro.11
The liberal soul shall be made Fat: for he that waters shall himself be watered.

Isa.16
God waters me with His tears!

Storage Battery

The physical body is a storage battery that contains two million live cells. These two million cells are magnetic and electric in relationship to each other and to the various functional organs of the body. They radiate life and act as a storage battery. The food that one eats keeps these cells fully charged and ready for activity.

But over-eating (surfeiting), along with years of undigested meals, depletes this charge, slowing everything down and making everything sluggish. This is also why Fasting is so important: it brings you back to Zero Ground (totally empty) and ready for the blood belly and body blood to be reloaded and charged for the Work of the Lord.

The maintenance of these cells does not require much food on a freshly reloaded body. Very often, they are over-charged because of over-eating, and when over-charged, they are less effective. Over-eating chokes the effective activity of these cells. I try to drink more water than the food I am eating. Water is more vital than food!

A car battery will not charge itself without enough water in it.

Exercise

Exercise is critical in balancing the slow mode that the body is in and stimulating the organs to keep them regular. Like water, these two ingredients are essential for the recipe of Fasting. You might not be able to exercise in the first 4-7 Fasts, but it will come as the toxic waste level comes down and the cleansing goes up.

"He must increase, and I must decrease".

Being diligent with water (blood needs lots), exercising 1-2 times a day (walking and biking will be a comfort), and refreshing the mind and body (even though you do not feel like it at the time – just try it and see.) I exercised almost every day of a 36 day Fast: sometimes up to an hour! The seasoned Faster will be able to get most things done in a day as the Faster matures in Fasting (cleansing – low toxic level). This does not include heavy work like carpenters. You would have to do a partial Fast, which is just as hard, if not harder, for the belly never falls asleep on a partial Fast and never reaches Zero Ground (total cleansing).

Pores of the skin

There is a lot of deep cleansing going on in a Fast that manifests undesirable odours appear in a Fast, manifesting from the pores of the skin and tongue. These odors will come to nothing as you continue to Fast, bringing down the toxic waste level. Regular washing and brushing of teeth and tongue will take care of that. The skin also becomes dry, which is par for the Course. Bathing provides a big drink for the body as well: the pores of the body take in water, allowing a greater intake of water. A consistently large volume of water is needed to dilute the toxic waste that is eradicated by the minute from your body, balance the body's negative energies, and relieve stress.

When Fasting, all the senses become sensitive in the holy flesh. Fasting sharpens the ears and the Sword of the Spirit (retaining Wisdom). It is one thing to get Wisdom, but another thing to retain it: to keep Wisdom on Your lips, fitted for Your mouth, as a precious Jewel for the "putting off the body, the sins of the flesh."

Gases

Some people, when they pass the wind, smell like someone died. That is because they have, a long time ago, because of the toxic waste level of undigested foods. A Clean Interior delivers a clean gas release of the body. When the digestive tract and the blood are cleansed, there should be a regular activity of gas release, for all food intakes. You would be surprised at the amount of gas buildup in the body from just one tea when in Zero Ground.

With solids there is a much quicker response time of gas when food is digested, while the belly is waking up during the Break of the Fast. Burps are thick, long, and deep, almost right after eating, when coming out of the "Break" (Zero Ground). But as the Harness of God comes off (eating the way You want): the gases dwindle down to almost nothing as the food intake gets bigger and richer over 3 or 4 months. Not a good sign.

Then, it is time for a trip into the Wilderness (Fasting) again!

Flehm

You will be coughing up flehm (with spots) quite frequently, on and off the Fast. In the early years of Fasting, the mucous was dark and spotted, much more concentrated, but as the toxic level comes down, the flehm becomes clearer and less frequent, then do nothing (deep cleansing)!

The mouth is the main vent of the body, and again, "the power of life and death is in the tongue, and they that love (respect-tame - Fast) it, will eat the Fruit (Life) of it."

Nose

The lifetime of toxic food waste finds its way out of every opening of the body, including the nose, filtering out to the fine hairs of the nostrils. There is a lot of mucous that comes from the nose when you are Fasting. The blood is extracting all waste out of every opening of the body, including the fine hairs of your nostrils. Sometimes there are big loads of mucous as it comes from the lowest recesses of the Interior. You will be picking the nose more often than usual because of the deep cleansing process.

Urine

There is lots of dark, heavy urine that appears after the belly falls asleep. A very deep, constant cleansing in this stage by the minute. The body needs time to export waste when surfeiting (over-eating), and missing a few meals will allow time for long, full stream, frequent urinating, and release of gases, thus, a total digestive resolution of the food intake.

A clean Interior is very responsive to food outcome if allowed the time. The urine should flow without any restriction whatsoever, and the same with the stool. This is also the working of the holy flesh, a disciplined body. You do not want to be delaying the digestive work of the holy flesh by over-eating!

Stool

About 4-5 days into the Fast, there's a natural enema takes place, with a flush of watery stool, right after entering Zero Ground (food particles and miscellaneous particles gone). In the early years of Fasting, there will be colon discomfort from all the toxic waste leaving the colon.

Flushing out the body 3 days before the Fast with lots of water and winding down food intake with vegetables - to fruit - to juice will make a huge difference in the discomfort of bowel movement and belly cramps the first few Fasts, and a complete difference as tox-level comes down. This kind of taming (Fasting) of the tongue will make Your wholesome (tamed) tongue a tree of Life, with your Words of Wisdom as the fruit of the tree.

Pro. 10
The tongue of the Righteous brings forth Wisdom.
(Which is the most valuable thing on the planet) .

Rage

As the battle rages, the devil pursues every avenue to break your will and tarnish the integrity of your Fast (Faith). Wrestling with the devil and your flesh can be exhausting, manifesting in rage. The Fast poking you all day, and at times all night, for 21 days: yes, you just might snap! And it could be over the smallest thing because, like a pressure cooker, it has been building up. It is par for the Course! Do not worry about it.

The arena of Fasting provides many opportunities for warfare, stepping up the Battle as the Lord of Hosts trains your hands for war and your fingers to fight with the Sword of the Spirit!

This steady warfare can wear down even the greatest of the Mighty, including Elijah, running from just some Jezebel. I have only experienced rage 3 times in my 58 Fasts. It has been a long time since I have experienced rage. It was only in the earlier years of Fasting.

Sleep

Sleep is the body's best friend. There are many benefits of sleep both spiritual and physical. Sleep is God's circuit breaker on sin for man, lest he continue therein and shorten his already few days upon the earth. The best thing to do when losing a fight in the Great Battle is to shut it down and go to sleep then regroup. The battle is in the flesh, and if You shut it down, there is no more fight!

Scattered sleep is par for the course in the early stages of Fast cleansings due to high levels of toxic waste. After timely, repeated cleansings (as the tox level comes down), the evolved holy flesh will sleep like a baby and belong to have Breakfast with the Lord in the morning, sitting under His shadow with great delight!

You get a wonderful, deep, content sleep in Fasting that is almost euphoric as you mature in Fasting (lower tox-level); you will lay yourself down in both safety and peace as the Lamp of the Lord passes through the midst of the Sacrifice (holy flesh). Just like Abraham in his "deep sleep" when cutting the Covenant of Jehovah.

True and false hunger

False Hunger

They are enclosed (imprisoned) in their own fat: with their mouth they speak proudly.

Most people have no idea about true and false hunger because they have no idea about Fasting.

False hunger only lasts 15 – 20 minutes (on a loaded belly and blood), and then it goes away. It is a false hunger because it goes away

Whenever the intestines stretch or shrink, there is discomfort, which is mistaken for true hunger.

Most people think the first shrink (pain) of the belly to be hunger, but it is not, It is only the first recoil (pain) of the intestines. True hunger is usually the 2nd or 3rd stomach pain, depending on how big the last meal was. A major meal with meat will require about 20-24 hours to digest, or the 3rd to 4th stomach pain. The one that does not go away!

A person could eat as much as he wanted, and whatever he wanted without gaining weight by this technique of eating from true hunger to true hunger
You do not eat until true hunger arrives, again.

True Hunger

True hunger has a greater kickback than false hunger, depending on the diet (meat and sugar). Meat has a harder kickback on the intestines than other foods and takes longer to digest. It would be Wise to wean off the meat before a Fast for less pain.

When entering the Fast, true hunger does not go away and stays until the stomach falls asleep, which could be 4 to 7 days – depending on how dirty the belly. Once Zero Ground (empty belly) is obtained, eating from true hunger to true hunger will keep all the weight and fat off, no matter what you eat.

Because you're eating from a full belly to a true resolve of total digestion of the last meal instead of it being pushed aside to accommodate the next premature, unnecessary food intake, this pushed aside waste compounds quickly into all kinds of undesirables. Fasting will quickly and specifically distinguish between true and false hunger because of Your constant, conscious location from Zero Ground (the Break of the Fast).

Food Intake

Blessing Your food has an entirely different meaning now! You bless that natural food, holy, every time! You bless that Spiritual food, holy, every time! Bless (sanctify) it wholly for your body, soul, and Spirit for its Divine Design!

The Lord adds or subtracts as body and soul need. Bless that meal with Faith and thanksgiving for the Divine Design every time! God can compensate for all deficiencies in the body and soul through divine providence, flipping the desires of the soul to taste the right decisions and keep you in times of famine.

The food absorption rate is slow in waking up the belly; the Faster does not want any excess food in the reload of the blood and digestive tract. The blood is a major reload itself, so give it plenty of time with natural pure foods, and follow the Break Schedule very carefully.

Piecing (eating) between meals will have an avalanche effect on more food.

You need to pull back and move the feeds to 5-hour intervals just to play it safe. Food output and intake inventory from Zero Ground will keep a conscious digestive tract, to know the top, middle, and bottom of the belly (with its Living waters)! When in the neighborhood of Zero Ground, there's total absorption of the meal for the most part, if no snacking between 4-5 hours intervals of meals. (interrupting the digestive process).

This is how you know you're in the neighborhood of Zero Ground, all the time, if that is where you want to be, maintaining Your holy flesh (Wisdom) all the time. Fasting is profoundly serious and a grave Work for the Kingdom of God!

Food Compass

The food compass is your constant, conscious location to Zero Ground and when to eat and not to eat.

It is now easy to monitor the food intake from a clean, empty belly because there is nothing in it. When you lose this tally of the food intake, it is time to Fast because the holy flesh has passed away from you. Servants of the Lord need to maintain their body with the holy flesh (Fasting), as they maintain their soul with the Bread of Life, as they maintain their spirit with the Blood of Jesus!

Your food compass (when to eat and not to eat) has been buried all this time in the Fast by not using it for a season. So, it is hard to tell when you are full or not because you have never reloaded an empty belly and blood before. This is the purpose of the Break Schedule. It is your temporary food compass. The Break Schedule (up ahead) must be concrete.

Maintaining the integrity of the small Fast is the same as the long Fast.

Therefore, the Break Schedule must be concrete!

The Pullback

Pulling back usually takes about 24 hours (with meat) to get back to Zero Ground.

There should not be much bowel movement. There should be almost total absorption of each meal when reloading the new Wineskin. The Faster needs to be able to discern between hunger pain and stomach recoil. Skip the next feed for a finer resolution of the digestion. Juicing (fresh blends) until feeling normal physically and emotionally will resolve everything.

Foolish mistakes come from being off guard because of the disposition of the outer man and the many distractions of the sufferings and labors of love.

Most of the time, I see the evil coming from a distance and hide Myself.

Food Outcome

If You cannot stop urinating, it is a sign of way too much food intake! Pull back toward Zero Ground by missing a few meals, until true hunger returns, as it always does. The food absorption rate is very thorough and slow when waking the stomach, and you do not want any excess food or elimination. No stool is a good sign of total absorption. Urine flow should be invited, full flow and gold.

There is still interior cleansing going on, which is another reason for going extremely slow. You are rebuilding the foundation of your belly and blood that the food float will ride upon. You are rebuilding a foundation for your new Wineskin and a whole heart that will manifest Your inheritance, the Christ in You, Your hope of glory.

Watch for the relationship between food intake and the body venting its gases.

Layer upon layer, step by step, inch by inch!

Physical back lag.

Surfeiting (over-eating) always brings a physical and Spiritual back lag to the body, soul, and spirit: because the life force of the body (blood) is polluted, delivering negative energies instead of positive energies. Manifesting in stress, fear, deception, scattered sleep, and all kinds of deficiencies,

"turning the Sweet (the Inner) into the bitter (outer)."

This is when it is time to Fast again, flipping the bitter to the Sweet! I believe that every Fast (new Wineskin) is uniquely custom-made for every individual by the Father, just like a person's fingerprint and Salvation.

Minimum stool = total absorption = successful Reload

You want minimum bowel movements; with total absorption of every meal during the Break by allowing time and space for food to digest efficiently. This is the physical Path of the Ancients, living from true hunger to true hunger and maintaining the holy flesh by Fasting. Every time the Faster gets into the Zero Ground ("the Zone"), it takes more Land (the Christ in You) in its refining process of the holy flesh.

Isa. 4
By the Spirit of burning (cleansing) and by the Spirit of judgment (making the right decisions).

Wondering where all the glory is?

It is in the new Wineskin, which is in Fasting and the keeping of His word (the daily Feeds).

Spiritual Back Lag

God periodically shuts down everything (Fasting) by Divine providence so He can speak and minister to You. To get you to be still, and to reflect on the Path: to hear and to carefully consider your Way! It could be up to 2 weeks before reaching the heights of Zion (the blessings)! Sometimes, there is a delay in the blessings for the harmonization of the body, soul, and Spirit, sometimes up to the same length of time as your complete Fast.

God safeguarding the blessing and takes the credit for the Fast:
and not you: lest You be puffed up in thinking "God owes me".

Sometimes the Faster, trying to justify all the constant disposition of his holy flesh for so long, will subconsciously expect immediate payment of some kind from God, for all the suffering, and that cross being carried can manifest itself in all kinds of pride and stress! But the strength of understanding of the Inner man cuts through all that like a Sword.

A lot of pride can set in from Fasting from revelations and quick growth and willpower when needed. The outer man will lead over the inner Man and make a mess, as usual, if the pride is not tempered with the meditation of the Word of His power. The blessing is because of the goodness of God; not My works or labors of Love (sufferings)!

Food Float

The food float is the food that rides on top of the clean foundation of the reloaded belly and blood.

It's important to lay a pure foundation of live, fresh, raw (blended) fruits and vegetables of different colors for nutrients, according to the Break Schedule. After you holy reload the belly and blood, all other foods just float around on top of the pure foundation in the process of elimination.

Like the bubbles of a pop riding on top of the drink that quickly disperse (true hunger to true hunger), so, it doesn't matter what you eat on top of the pure foundation because it quickly dissipates from the quick, clean, efficient response of the holy flesh (clean Interior). Now, you can go from true hunger to true hunger (bubbles disappearing) without putting on any weight! The experienced Faster will keep the Break going as long as possible; the longer, the better, for a smooth transition from the Break to regular eating. If you over-eat to the full, it will be 20 hrs. of rough backtracking to the last meal. You will always know when you are cutting into the holy flesh (the Foundation). Even when I AM not Fasting and eating what I want, there is a conscious inventory of everything going into the mouth from Zero Ground (the Break). This Harness of God that is on my tongue allows Jesus to "feed Me with food that is convenient for Me, lest I be full and deny Him."

Even in My eating season, I find My body (new Wineskin) resolving Itself on its own, conflict-free through skipped meals, to avoid surfeiting.

There is a imitate relationship now between you and your body. After a short time of eating, I back off on food intake for more water intake. You adopt a holy eating lifestyle through Fasting.

Now I know how much salt –sugar, etc. I will be taken in and can compensate by digestive resolution (waiting for true hunger) – waiting a little longer for digestion to catch up. Now, by eating at true hunger, I can eat till I am full, then eat again at true hunger, which is usually every 4-6 hours (if not snaking), for all this food will be mostly absorbed

because of a quick responsive digestive tract, and a clean Interior. A clean Interior brings an immediate and thorough response to the food intake: no sludge gumming up the gears of digestion and gas release.

The Holy Ghost needs to reveal Himself in a holy Body; He wants to resonate the Interior and permeate the exterior (holy flesh). True and false hunger will help to properly monitor your Interior from Zero Ground. Zero Ground is the key to holy eating. It is extremely important to know when to allow digestive resolution by missing again, the meals required to stay in the neighborhood of Zero Ground,

Waiting for the cycle of true hunger (3rd or 4th hunger pain) to return, according to its custom.

This is extremely important! The belly needs time to expand and absorb, for it is now waking up. Once your food intake is entirely accomplished, the food floating on top of this foundation will not matter much, for it will be consumed in the faithful cycle of true hunger!

A SPIRITUAL MATURITY IS SETTING IN, WITH A READINESS TO AVENGE ALL DISOBEDIENCE.

When it comes to the belly, it is far better for a larger output than input, for higher efficiency, because from the belly flows rivers of Living waters: not your head.

Pro. 14
A sound heart (clean blood) is the life of the flesh (holy flesh),

Jn. 4
... from your belly shall flow rivers of Living waters.

The prime directive for Fasting is a whole heart (which = body, soul, spirit, and blood) to create an atmosphere (holy flesh which = both interior and exterior) that is conducive to the Holy Spirit, the Fruit giver.

Mt. 3:3

MAKE STRAIGHT IN THE WILDERNESS (FASTING) A HIGHWAY FOR OUR GOD.

When it comes to Fasting, blessing, and promotion, do not come cheap because you're dealing with the refining of the body and soul to complete purity through the holy flesh (the Circumcision of Christ) and the Word that became flesh. Which is very possible, even here in this world; even today: even right now, for We are complete in Him (holy flesh).i When the Faster has the belly (food) under control, he may then move on to Fasting the tongue (words).

Deuteronomy 32

For the Lord alone did lead him, and there was no strange god in him. He made him ride on the high places of the earth, that he might eat the increase of the fields.

He made him to suck honey out of the rock, and oil out of the flinty rock. Butter of cattle, the milk of sheep, with the fat of lambs, and rams of the breed of Bashan, and goats with the "fat of kidneys of wheat"; You did drink the pure blood of the Grape,

Eze. 34
Even the Heritage of Jacob, to Feed upon those goodly fat pastures, upon the high mountains of Israel.

Fasting produces great willpower, which in return produces great Faith because of all their many similarities. Faith through the arena of Fasting forges a two-edged Sword in your hand that divides the flames of fire. Nothing is impossible with these two ingredients of the Divine Design, the Christ in You, Your hope of glory! The holy flesh (the Circumcision of Christ) flourishes in Fasting, causing the scope of your Faith to see beyond the natural into the impossible. Nothing is impossible for a Man or Woman of God with a whole heart, whose Words from a tamed tongue and clean blood (the Spirit) execute the judgment written about anything of God's Word and Realm: for both for himself, his neighbor, and for the common good of all.

The total cost of the Fast financially = $40 for juice - fresh fruit and vegetables in the Break.

The total cost of the Fast Spiritually =   the whole body, soul, and spirit (blood).

Chapter 8

"Breaking the Fast" (The Break)

For a 1 week Fast:
7 days for body recovery.
Another 7 days for soul recovery!
Another 7 days for full recovery!!

I have to admit it's a long way back to a fully loaded body, but well worth a brand-new blood, belly, soul (a whole heart), and an iron will that spills over into every aspect of your life reigning as a king on the throne of my heart.

You will be coming out the Fast the same way you went in, suffering because of stretching of the intestines and the cravings of the mind, with a grumbling stomach and discomfort, even slight cramps in the belly will come, and the mind just roaring to get to regular eating. but all worth the "New You," that will spring forth like the Dawning of the morning.

A lot of resistance will be required in the Break because you are now taking in a small amount of nutrition, but you still have to wait another week before regular eating, which will make you very anxious to go to regular eating.

The idea is total food absorption and fewer bowel movements for maximum efficiency in the re-loading of the blood and body. There is still interior cleansing going on during the Break until the body is fully re-loaded, and then the cleansing comes down to almost nothing when fully reloaded, which is another reason Fasting is so important.

Remember:

The book of Deuteronomy Ch. 17 tells us that the life of the flesh is in the blood.

Chapter 12 also tells us that the life of the soul is also in the blood. That means the life of your feelings – thoughts – will –and imagination are in your blood.

Bad blood = bad soul and bad body.

Pro. 14
A sound heart (clean blood) is the life of the flesh (holy flesh).

IT IS IMPORTANT TO KEEP THIS IN MIND WHEN RELOADING THE BLOOD AND BODY.

Faithful in the Break of a small Fast = Faithful in the Break of a long Fast.

We need to consider future restraint, for the future long Fast!

THIS IS EXTREMELY IMPORTANT: DAMAGE COULD OCCUR FROM BREAKING A LONG FAST THE WRONG WAY!

SLOW TIMELY FOOD INTAKE = TOTAL FOOD ABSORPTION = COMFORTABLE BOWEL MOVEMENTS = SUCCESSFUL BREAK.

This is where the Men are separated from the boys! All the Ancients of the Lord and the Disciples stood under the pressure of the Battle (Fasting). The Father will test every man's mettle with salt and fire (Fasting)!

The "Break" is the hardest and most important part of the Fast. This reload of the body is the foundation of your whole life (body and soul - thoughts – feelings, etc.).

It's wake up time for everybody!

The stomach and tongue (taste buds) have been hibernating all this time (even in a short 7-day fast.) It is going to take a lot more time than you think or feel to wake everybody up, especially those delicate little fine hairs of the belly called "Cilia", which are slow in waking up, there being so many of them.

Your "Cilia" - millions of fine hairs that push the food along - need a lot of space and time to wake up. They all need to be awake and active before regular eating. Most of the Interior has been hibernating, except the blood (which has sped up). There are a lot of things to wake up, to get going, and to fill up.

Imagine a very old man waking up in the morning. You want to take it easy on him and give him all the time he needs. Waking up the belly is like warming up the engine of the car in extremely cold weather; you do not want to be driving it before the engine is ready.

You could break something!

You do not want to be putting sugar (regular eating) into the tank of a car, gumming up the gears!

THE RELOADING OF THE BLOOD AND THE BODY ARE AT STAKE.
YOU COME TOO FAR NOW TO THROW IT ALL AWAY!

Time is critical:

Time is critical for the belly's resolve and the balancing of the Interior to keep the integrity of the will (throne) glorious and intact and to keep the Living waters flowing,

SO, PUT ON THE BRAKES! KEEP THEM ON! AND WATCH OUT!

The objective of the Break is to reload the blood and body in the designated time frame of the "Break" and Food Schedule. for maximum absorption of all food intake, and for maximum efficiency of digestion. (This is more time added on to the Fast).

REMEMBER:

You are coming out the same way you went in; with hunger pains (intestines stretching) and discomfort, to allow time for total absorption and fill up. So, get comfortable with the idea of suffering again, and it will go a lot easier on your mind.

2 Tim. 2
For if We suffer with Him: We will also reign with Him.

So, count the Cost!

GO VERY, VERY, SLOW.

Consider this:

You will lose 18 hours of digestive resolve (discomfort and loss of integrity) for 1 handful of solid food if you go ahead of the Food Schedule. Definitely not worth the backtrack! Do not be pulling another Esau, who squandered his Inheritance for a "dainty morsel" and sought repentance afterward.

Ecc. 4

The fool folds his hands and eats his own flesh!

Right now, I'm on the second day of the break of this 36 day Fast and writing this chapter; comfortably! I am 2 days on 4 oz. of juice diluted to 8 oz. every 4 hours – 3 servings only.

Next 2 days 8 oz. regular juice - every 4 hours (5 better) – Only 3 servings a day (belly is satisfied).

P.S.

The "Break" of the Fast is overwhelming, but it is harnessed by the value of the interior cleanse (the New Man).

There was a time in my early years of Fasting when those sizzling, dainty morsels of food were mountainous! But now they are just a tiny, distant voice in the wind that I can hardly hear or see!

The "Time Frame"

(See Break Schedule page 87)

This time frame will guarantee a safe break from the Fast!

There must be an absolute, concrete resolve to this "Break Schedule" – both time and food, against all appearances and feelings. You need to curb your desires and allow yourself to be fed with food that is convenient for Me, lest I be full and deny Him.

The body needs a certain amount of time to absorb and digest the food (internal resolution): Trying to speed up the process will not change that; it will only destroy what you are building: just not worth it.

Pro. 20
Bread gained by deceit is sweet to a man, but afterwards it will be as gravel in the mouth!

Coming out of the Fast is very disorientating because your "food compass" has been buried for a while, so it needs to be concrete according to time. The Break Schedule, not feelings!

Just like Faith – We do not walk by Our senses.

Your "food compass" (knowing when to eat and not to eat) has been buried by the Fast; determining true and false hunger can be complicated, particularly coming out of a long Fast (14 days or longer). Reloading the outer man is like digging up a valuable archaeological find. You need to excavate very carefully and slowly so as not to ruin the Find (a new Wineskin - Christ in You) with a wrong reload of body and blood. The integrity of the Break of a small Fast should be the same as a long Fast. Even though it was just a small Fast, you need to consider the Break of a long Fast. You could do some damage coming out of a major Fast (3 weeks and longer) the wrong way.

A long Fast needs steadfast integrity to break it properly and safely this steadfast. There must be a serious attitude toward this schedule, for it is your digestive compass, and it will prevent you from much discomfort.

Your body must slowly absorb nutrients; the belly is waking ("the cilia hairs") up. So, most of the early break feels unsatisfied it seems you still feel hungry, but your body and blood are still loading at a slow, efficient pace!

The Break Schedule must be concrete!

When exiting a Fast, there is a certain "Time Frame" the body needs to reload itself back to normal. Eating more than the "Time Frame" allows only brings unresolved blood, discomfort, and loss of time. The whole body is filling up again and it needs a lot of time.

Once again, you must be faithful and careful, with all diligence, to maintain the Break Schedule!

Like Faith. you cannot rely on the senses. Your body is totally empty of nutrition, and the stomach has been lying dormant.

Remember:
You have never reloaded your blood and belly before!

Rushing this process is not even an option;
it will not fix anything!

That which goes through the fire (suffering for His namesake) is purged to complete purity! There is a lot more reloading than you think. Much time is needed to reload. You cannot judge by your feelings (same as Faith) because you have never reloaded your body before. So, it must be reloaded by Faith (The Break Schedule – not your feelings).

There is a very strong tendency to rush this time-food interval! So, stick to the Break Schedule!

The lengthy repercussions and the amount of holy Ground lost from breaking the "Schedule" the wrong way - is not worth the noticeably short time of relief and a tainted reload of the body and soul.

Just not worth it!

A scary testimony!

Let me tell you about a serious scare I had in my early days of Fasting when my toxic waste level was still high.

It was about my 10th Fast or so, and in the middle of a 14-day Fast, I had a meal of 2 scrambled eggs and 2 potatoes. As soon as I finished, I had hot and cold flashes, vomiting, and My head started spinning for about 10 minutes, which seemed like a lifetime.

All this winded down after about 20 minutes and I was ok and went on to finish the Fast. The Holy Spirit reassured me that I was safe in His arms.

There are certain liberties a seasoned Faster has over the amateur Faster because of a low toxic waste level. But now I can have a small cheeseburger in the middle of a 10-day Fast and sneak by with little discomfort. This is because I've gone down from a 100% toxic waste level to a 20% toxic level (clean interior).

Everyone starts at 100% toxic because of a lifetime of unresolved digestion of meals!

This was the only episode of 63 Fasts.

Pro.12
There shall no evil happen to you, neither shall any plague come near your dwelling.

THE BREAK SCHEDULE

Remember!
Same amount of break days as the Fast before regular eating!

7-day Fast = 7-day Break!

There is still cleansing going on, a natural scraping from the fiber of fresh, live raw food of different colors for different nutrients! Feel free to vary the drink and food but stay in its category.

There will be 3 servings a day - at 4-hour intervals - for both short and long fasts.

The Short Fast

(3 to 7 days)

Day 1

Fresh squeezed Juice (antioxidants)

9:00 am - 8 ounces of fresh juice - (pomegranate recommended)

1:00 pm - 8 ounces of fresh juice - tomato

5:00 pm - 8 ounces of fresh juice – blackberry

Day 2

Fresh raw fruit

9:00 am   - small bowl

1:00 pm   -   medium bowl

5:00 pm   - large bowl

Day 3

Fresh raw vegetables

9:00 am   - small bowl

1:00 pm   -   small bowl

5:00 pm   - medium bowl

Day 4

Breads and dairy (no condiments till regular eating)

9:00 am   -   medium bowl or plate

1:00 pm   -   large bowl or plate

5:00 pm   -   large bowl or plate

Day 5

Breads and grains (no condiments till regular eating)

9:00 am   -   medium bowl or plate

1:00 pm   -   large bowl or plate

5:00 pm   -   large bowl or plate

Day 6

Anything but meat (no condiments till regular eating)

9:00 am   -   medium bowl or plate

1:00 pm   -   large bowl or plate

5:00 pm   -   large bowl or plate

Day 7

BACK TO REGULAR EATING.

If you over eat, it will take about 16 to 24 hours to resolve the digestive process; just not worth it!

The Medium Fast

(7 to 14 days):

SAME AS THE SHORT BREAK BUT HALF THE FOOD INTAKE

(Dilute juices with water)

The Long Fast

(21 to the return of hunger in the belly)

SAME AS THE MEDIUM BREAK BUT ONE THIRD THE FOOD INTAKE

(Dilute juices with water)

Back to regular eating and maintenance of the holy flesh and a daily holy eating lifestyle with Jesus as Lord of your food.

Eventually, the Holy Ghost will customize your Break to suit your metabolism, For everybody's metabolism is different: fearfully and wonderfully made!

Let me say it one more time:

There are a lot of things to wake up, to get going, and to fill up.

THE RELOADING OF THE BLOOD AND THE BODY ARE AT STAKE. YOU'VE COME TOO FAR NOW TO THROW IT ALL AWAY!

There is a triune resolve in the "Break" :

Phase 1 (body)

Reloading body and blood

Juice – vegetable – live fresh – dairy – breads – grains

Phase 2 (soul)

If you do a 21-day fast, it will be 21 more days before your body re-establishes itself back to normal and it may be another 21 days before you are emotionally reloaded.

Phase 3 (spirit)

The tongue has been refreshed in power, so take advantage of the power in it.

Look to follow through in prayers and meditation; the Stage has been set.

Pro. 18
A man's belly shall be filled by the fruit of his mouth, and by the increase of his lips he shall be filed For the power of life and death is in the tongue.

Pro.15
A wholesome (tamed) tongue is a Tree of life, but crookedness in it is a breach in the spirit.

Fast Tracking Chart

(This is one of My tracking-chart. Just erase information and put yours in, as a new template.)

DAY 1

Physical Status

Food Intake

8:00 am - nothing

12:00 pm - nothing

4:00 pm - nothing

Food output

Urine

lots - full stream – no problem

Gases

lots – hard and deep - lots of flam form mouth and mucous from nose stool

Stool

watery - a little discomfort about 10 minutes

Flehm

throat -lots   nose – above average

Water

3 pints

Energy

50% - swimming

Sleep

Nice - no interruptions

Physical Comments

Spiritual Status

The Word - mine

Hosea 1-6

Jaylah

        Done See Jays Word schedule in ("Fresh Manna" file)

Jah

        Done - see – Eternal Confessions for the little Lambs ("Fresh Manna" file)

Mediation

        The Cry #6 – Wisdom #2

Worship

        Old Rugged Cross – He Knows My name – I will serve you

Prayer

        Psalms 119

Labors of love

        Helped with neighbors garage – and the kids' spiritual feed

Spiritual Comments

Good and bad comforts.

Good Comforts:

Meditation of the Word and Worship

In the early years of Fasting, much time is spent resisting food temptations, which eventually dwindle down to almost nothing as the spirit and soul get used to functioning without food. Meditation of the Word will feed the mind with hope and faith that will outweigh the food temptations and any other temptations, for the Word of God is alive, quick, and powerful. Do not underestimate the power of meditation – Your shield against the flesh and the spirit of Mammon. Meditation (roasting) of the Word never fails!

Fellowship

Fellowship is Divine when Fasting because of your holy connection and Identification with the Body of Christ. You feel with Your keen senses the Christ in Them (or not). Fellowship of any kind will immediately distract you from the Battle at hand.

Pro. 27
"As iron sharpens iron, so one man sharpens another."

Labors of love

Are paramount in any activity of the Christian life. It is supreme and trumps everything, for God is love.

Be ready for every work to the glory of God, for it is more blessed to give than receive. Just try it and see!

Exercise

This is where you need to step out in Faith past the weakness. Once you start exercising, you will start to feel better. Just try it and see! Exercise is a great stress reliever, as the mind is now otherwise occupied. Exercise stimulates the blood, digestion system, and other vital parts of the body. Exercising also distracts the mind from any ongoing mental traffic!

Bath

It is a challenge drinking a lot of water on a Fast. Bathing provides a big drink for the body through the pores of the skin. Bathing provides an easy large volume of water intake. There's just something about the belly lying in hot water that is very soothing. I take 2-3 of them a day when Fasting.

Sleep

There is a deeper cleansing during sleep, which is evident in the huge amount of flehm (interior waste) as soon as you wake up that comes out of your mouth, along with the many other flehms while you are awake.

There is nothing wrong with taking a few short naps during Fasting. It's your ace in the hole against the Devil and the flesh.

Sleep shuts down the Battle that was raging!

Bad Comforts:

It is very important to note that bad comforts during Fasting will put you into deeper bondage, just like good comforts sets you freer! This is why it is important to have a total resolve of commitment in your heart before Fasting!

Fasting amplifies everything!

CONSIDER CAREFULLY THE DAMAGES OF BAD COMFORTS WHEN FASTING.

Old bad habits are easy to suppress while Fasting because the flesh has no gas to fuel the habit.

It is easy to fall back into the old comforts of the flesh when under stress and pressure, but the Truth of the matter is that it simply boils down to making a decision (executing judgment). If you are sincere for the good, you will have the good.

Television – (or anything worldly)

Jer. 9
Death has sneaked in through our windows (WIFI): it has entered our fortresses, cutting off children from the streets and young men from the squares.

The internet - TV. can easily "sneak in through the windows" (WIFI) to consume all your time.

A direct line (feed) from the world providing an avenue of ample feed (unbelief), that will crush the inner Man, turning the Sweet (Christ) to the bitter (world and flesh), shouldering out worship, the Word, labors of love, and precious family time. WIFI will conform you to this world instead of Christ: The world cares nothing for the things of God, and to be friends with this world is to be an enemy of God. We are to be in the world, but not of it, "for a friend of fools shall be destroyed" (Pro. 13:20).

Too much worldly influence will pollute your Spiritual inheritance! T.V. - Google influences a wide array of feelings. A collage of lying, scoffing, and folly with a distorted view of Truth. WIFI – Google (the Tree of the Knowledge of Good and Evil) delivers a great payload of folly that chokes the Word of His power. T.V. can be effective and productive if used Wisely and not for too long.

You want to make sure that the light that is in you is not darkness! This deceit will lead to falsehood and your whole life a lie without God. The Eye (spirit) needs to be single, "for the spirit of a man is the Lamp of the Lord". The Eye is the light of the body and needs to be kept single, aimed at the Target (Word) of Life: or how great will that darkness be when the Light (the Word) is replaced with the darkness (things) of this world?

Fornication

Fornication is the one thing We are to flee from, according to the Bible, which speaks of its grave seriousness. Concerning everything else, we are to stand and then stand some more to the very end. When Fasting, everything seems trivial and insignificant compared to having a loaded body with full strength and peace. The zest of the flesh is absent, and the sex organ is just as out of Place as the body is. The libido is in low mode as the mind and body are.

Fornication happens because of stress build-up (in or out of the Fast). Sex is a popular way to release stress. Sex is a result of a Spiritual disposition, not a physical one, for in the holy flesh, there is no stimulation of the sexual organ, except manually simulated by yourself. Do not be discouraged because of a single loss in the Battle of Life. The body has become Your slave because of all those many, many no's in just one of Fast.

Pro. 11
The fool (outer man) shall be servant to the Wise (Inner Man - Christ in You).

Fornication is a biggie in the Body of Christ, for nothing is ever said about it. The Body of Christ would be displaying much more holiness, glory, and power, if She were totally holy!

REMEMBER:
Do not be discouraged when you crash in Fasting; it is inevitable in your first dozen Fasts or so, but consider all the willpower that you have built up to now. Keeping your integrity and saying "no" under constant stress is outstanding!

Drugs

By the 5th day of the Fast everything is gone, including all drugs.

Drugs are crutches! The human body is fearfully and wonderfully made in the image and likeness of God and is entirely self-sufficient to sustain itself. If you can just give God half a chance by resisting (in any degree), the onslaught of the devil.

In other words, if you have a headache, don't take a Tylenol: pray instead, and give God half a chance to deliver you!

"We have not, because We ask not".

Negative People

It would be Wise in your early years of Fasting to stay out of the world (hang out in your prayer closet). The world system has a spiritual pull that will suck you in like a black hole, and when your blood and body is un-loaded, it is hard to resist.

For example: you do not want to go to the grocery store when you're on a Fast.

The world is the Devil's arena: try and stay out of it until you are re-loaded again. As a seasoned Faster (58 Fasts) I can do almost anything, go anywhere, and even cook meals for the family with no problem.

FASTING – Meditation #4 – The Glory

Theme

Mk. 2:20-22

But the days will come when the Bridegroom shall be taken away from Them,
Then, will They fast in those days.

No man sews a new piece of cloth on an old garment, for the new piece that filled it
takes away from the old and the rent is made worse.

No man puts new Wine into old bottles (skins): for the new Wine will burst
the bottles, and the Wine is spilled, and the bottles are marred,
but new Wine (Holy Spirit) must be put into
new Bottles (wine skins).

Eph. 5:18-20

Be not drunk with wine, but be filled with the Spirit, by speaking to Yourselves in Psalms,
hymns, and Spiritual songs, singing and making melody in Your heart unto the Lord.
(and Fasting to provide a new Wineskin for the New wine):

giving thanks always for all things to God and the Father,
in the Name of the Lord Jesus Christ;
and submitting Myself to God and My neighbor, in the fear of the Lord.

Introduction

Isa. 52:1-2

Awake, Awake; put on Your strength oh Zion!

Put on Your beautiful Garments, oh Jerusalem, the holy city; for there shall no more come into You the uncircumcised and the unclean.

Shake Yourself from the dust; arise and sit down, oh Jerusalem; loose Yourself from the bands of Your neck, oh captive Daughter of Zion.

Content

Isa. 58:6-1

This is the fast that God has chosen!

To loosen the bands of wickedness, to undo the heavy burdens,
To let the oppress go free, and that You break every yoke.

It is to deal My bread to the hungry, and that I bring the poor that are cast out to My house.
I will not hide Myself from My own flesh. and so, will My light break out as the morning,
and My health will spring forth speedily, and My righteousness will go
before Me, and the glory of the Lord will be My back-up!

Then I will call, and the Lord will answer, I will cry, and He will say "here I AM".
If I take away from the midst of Me the putting forth of the finger, and speaking vanities;

I will also draw out My soul to the hungry, to satisfy the afflicted soul;
My light will rise in obscurity, and My darkness as the noon day.

For the Lord is guiding Me continually, and satisfying My soul in drought, and making fat My bones:
I AM: like a watered Garden whose waters never fail I will observe the Sabbath: from doing
My own pleasure on His holy day, and call the Sabbath a delight, honorable;
I will honor Him, not doing My own ways,
nor finding My own pleasure, nor speaking My own words:

Then I will delight Myself in the Lord; and He will cause Me to ride upon the high places
of the earth, and feed Me with the Heritage (the Word of God)
of My father Jacob; for the mouth of the Lord has spoken it.

Ps 85

Yes, the Lord will give that which is good and Our land (heart - Christ in Me) will yield her increase!

Pro. 23:19

Hear My son, and be wise, and guide Your heart in the Way.
Be not among winebibbers; among riotous eaters of flesh:
For the drunkard and the glutton shall come to poverty,
and drowsiness will clothe a man of rags.

It is a good thing that the heart be established in grace;
not with meats, which have not profited them.

Ps. 78:18

They tempted God in their heart by asking for meat for their lust.

Pro. 21:23

I will keep My mouth (Words-confession);
I will keep My tongue (belly-fasting-blood),
and thereby keep Myself from all troubles.

S.O.S. 8:2

He has brought Me to His banqueting Table, and His banner over Me is Love.

Isa. 50:4

The Lord God has given me the tongue of the Learned.

Summary

Ps.111

The Lord has given Meat unto Me because I fear Him,
and He will be ever mindful of His covenant towards Me!

Ps. 23:5

The Lord is Our host spreading a feast for Us, while our foes look on.
You have poured oil on Our heads and Our cup runs over.

P.S.

Acts 15:28-29

The Holy Spirit and We (the 12 disciples) have decided not to impose
any extra burden (laws) on You, apart from these essential requirements:

1. Abstaining from food that is offered to idols.

2. Tasting the blood from the flesh of animals that have been strangled.

There are only three laws of the New Testament, and two of them are about food.

3. Keeping away from sexual vice.

KEEP AWAY FROM THIS AND YOU WILL PROSPER.

Chapter 9

Fasting for the Children!

To make sure their Temple of the Lord is holy (clean) and worthy of their "high calling" in Christ Jesus.

Pro. 24
Prepare your work without (Fasting - the flesh), and make it fit for the field (My heart): then afterwards, build My palace (the Christ in Me).

Pro. 14
A Wise woman builds her mansion: but the foolish plucks it down with their hands.

Pro. 18
The power of Life and death is in the tongue, and they that love it will eat the fruit of it.

Fasting has brought Me into a daily conscious attitude towards My Children's natural and Spiritual feed, which is paramount in My daily life and theirs: that they continue My spiritual throne and glory in the high calling of God, executing the judgments of the Lord.

There are 2 goals to keep in mind:

1st - New Wineskin – maintaining clean belly and blood (holy flesh).

2nd – A tamed tongue – controlling taste buds and straight and soft Words.

FASTING WILL DELIVER BOTH OF THEM.

Every Child has their own personal chef (parent, etc.) that feeds them daily. Sadly, to say most chefs know nothing about the children's Interior or Fasting, or how to reload an empty body and blood.

We need to establish a Fasting and holy eating lifestyle from the earliest of age, as parents bringing the Children up in the nurture (feeding the Bread of Life) and admonition (teaching) of the Lord: the earlier the better!

Starting the Child off right from a baby with healthy foods to establish healthy taste buds: Most parents start off this way but that does not last for long. The parents should get knowledge on healthy eating.

Lots of water (more than food).

Almond milk instead of cow milk. (Lasts for weeks without going bad)

Lots of grains (flax bread has a natural taste).

Lots of vegetables.

Natural granulated cane sugar (as much natural food as possible)

The best vitamin for the Child is vitamin "No."

It would be Wise to invest some time to research the different foods for the different benefits (food chart). After all, they only have one body for their one life on this planet. Since the power of life and death is in the tongue, it would be Wise to keep a tight leash on their tongue, with both food and Words, which, if done right, will be the hardest thing you ever do. A tamed tongue is awfully expensive on your soul!

You do not want their taste buds going wild on the fake food of this crooked world. Keep them in wholesome live foods and away from all the hard foods. Pump them with that vital vitamin "No." They will not even notice the difference in taste if you start them very early. This is also another phase of taming the tongue (taste buds).

It is very hard to reverse once taste buds are established, for the power of Life and death is in their tongue.

Get hold of their taste buds before the Devil does because he knows that if he has their tongue, he has them, for the power of their life is in the Child's tongue. Remember: their tongue is an unruly member that no man can tame. The parent should be gentle and diplomatic when it comes to Fasting for the Children.

Controlling the belly stretch of the children.

The best way to start is by setting an example for them, by skipping meals here and there, and letting them know that they are Fasting. This will build an association with Fasting by hearing about it and doing it, lodging it into their minds, which the Father may pull up anytime in their life. This will introduce them to an attitude of Fasting which the Lord will continue in their lives as they grow up.

Since the Children are Fasting (10-12 hours) all night when they sleep (by not eating), it is not that hard to add another 5 hours to their all-night Fast. Be gentle at first by adding only 5 hours in the morning; that way, they only miss breakfast. Then, eventually, add more according to their capacity. Do not concern yourself with their whining and complaining, for it is only for a short time, and they will not die but Live. Missing breakfast will not be all that hard for them, but when they start missing breakfast and lunch, they might act like they are going to die. Well, they will not. It is all a smoke screen to give in. Do not give in!

You are building up their muscle of Faith and training their hands for war and their fingers to fight. You will have to fill them up with water and vitamin "No," with a stressless, lovingly soft "No".

You gently keep adding hours as they become successful in their last Fast.

As the Fasts get longer, it is especially important that you be diplomatic (with straight and soft words) and adamant in character in the midst of their wagging, untamed tongue.

You do not want to cause any more stress than what is already there. Try and keep their mind off food by keeping it occupied – the Word, games, sports, etc. Give them a lot of water, and it will fill their little belly! Once they start Fasting the full day, it will be much harder on them, so we should be much more compassion with their sufferings. Allowing small amounts of food (piecing) to ease their suffering will be merciful and kind.

A glass of pure juice or a handful of fruit will be enough. Keep pushing their limits gently!

Keep in mind that the Children are on their way to Fasting for days and weeks in the coming future in their pursuit of their Divine Design, which should be more than enough inspiration for the fray of the Battle. It is hard enough doing your own Fasts, never mind carrying others on your back (Faith). It will be the most challenging you ever do, with the greatest glory, leaving them a great Inheritance (in Christ Jesus). You should also be praying for them behind the scenes for God's divine providence to secure the family's atmosphere with peace.

The Father will give you Wisdom in this in the pursuit of His divine design. It will be rough at first, but the Father will soon quicken both you and the Children for His high calling of Fasting!

You should always be in their Fast as a Fasting partner to encourage them by seeing you do it as well. They will eventually get used to Fasting, and they will appreciate the "turning of the bitter to the sweet". You will appreciate the fact that the Children are learning to discipline and maintain their holy flesh and are now having a relationship with their own bodies.

It's important that you have full control of the kitchen with strict enforcement. The parent needs to know exactly what and how much food their eating. This way, you can control their digestion resolution by allowing time between meals for full digestion.

We have Fasting Fridays at our house every other Friday, on our way to every Friday. We want to be constantly grooming their spirit (the Blood of Jesus – daily repentance), soul (the Word of His power), and body (Fasting – holy eating).

"Thank you Father God for this food and everything in my life.
I thank you for leading me into Fasting and a holy eating lifestyle.
Bless this food holy for my body Divine Design in Jesus' name.

The Rod of Reproof

The tamed tongue is the most effective tool for the Fasting of the physical body and the (outer man), and the Spiritual feed of the inner Man. Therefore, their tongue should be the main concern of the parent. The Children must fear the rod of your mouth before they can fear the rod (the Word) of God's mouth. Your Words should carry a loving graveness that makes your Words law!

Never let a command fall.

Your speech should be gentle with the law of kindness in your mouth, with a firm attitude, because you are setting the pace for future Fasts, which will require a serious No from you and a serious submission from them while considering the fact that they are already irritated from the Fast, and you do not want to add a bunch of hard and crooked words to their irritation.

No parent wants to see their little People suffering, so the parents will have to be very strong and courageous in their decisions, for a "Just man walks in his integrity and his Children are blessed after him"! Abraham, in his integrity to honor God in the sacrificing of his only son, put the fear of God into Isaac his son, which lasted unto his Children's children, and for generations, unto this day! You can be sure Isaac's ears went up when he heard the rod of Abraham's mouth, just like mine go up today at the Father's words of his mouth. You can be sure that Abraham never had to spank Isaac after that sacrificial scenario! If you start them off early enough with the rod of your mouth and maintain your integrity, So, that you will not have to spank them in the near future. The Father wants their conversation (lifestyle) of the Children ordered uprightly, and then the rest of their life will follow.

The integrity of their Fast (all the "No") will eventually spill over into every aspect of their life for success.

Fasting will play a major role in the taming of their tongues, which is crucial for the success of their life. For the power of Life and death is in the tongue, and they that love it (Life) will eat the fruit of it. Especially little Children, for their hearts are Innocent, and "theirs is the Kingdom of God."

P.S.

The Devil is on the sideline just waiting to take over their feed, for they are always being fed one way or another.

The world and the carnal flesh (base creature) are run by the Devil, "the prince of the air", trying to establish his feed for the outer man at the earliest of age through the airwaves (internet, television. etc.). Fasting is the quickest and easiest way to take the vile away from the precious. The other option is a long, drawn-out fight of trials and errors, taking a lifetime to sort out. Just 5 small years of Fasting did more for Me in the taking away (and understanding) of the vile than 30 years without Fasting.

Fasting deals with the interior (Tongue and Living waters), renovating the belly and blood for Living waters, and Taming the tongue so that it may bear the full weight of Wisdom! Fasting will totally shut down the outer man – reviving the "hidden Man of the heart", to subdue and lead (with gladness and joy) the outer man into the fat pastures (holy flesh) of God.

Ecclesiastes 16
He that labors works for himself; for his mouth craves it of him.

It has taken Me years of fasting, repenting – edging – curbing - corralling (the Children back to the Word all day), and weaving the Word into the vocabulary (true Taming of the tongue) to take away the vile from the precious; a blow for blow battle. Any kind of hardness and crookedness must be eradicated immediately by confession. Psalm 119 and the Proverbs will explain in full detail the hardness and the crookedness of the mouth and heart.

(see "Divine Blueprints for Meditation" for the Mouth 1 2 3 4.)

My Daughter of Zion (Jaylah)

In 2010, my heavenly Father led me to Ps.119 for integrity and holiness with all its many "I will," which led me to Fast with all it's many "No's," which led me to the Spiritual feed of my Children. All the holiness from Ps.119 and all the integrity from Fasting quickened me to see the need for my children's own spiritual feed, which has become paramount in Our lives.

It boggled my mind how I could be so Spiritual and at the same time be so blind to the Children's spiritual feed!

There is nothing more important in Our lives (except for Jesus) than their Spiritual feed, and they know it! I drill that doctrine deep into her soul!

Parents need to swallow the fact that Children need to eat Spiritually every day. Their inner Man needs to eat the Bread of Life every day, 3 times a day (60 minutes broken down into 3 rounds of 20 minutes), is enough to feed the Christ in Them - Their hope of glory! Before you know it, years go by, and the Feed goes on, and the Fruit of the Spirit keeps coming forth. For they are working the "common Faith" (the Word of His power) that is in them through the Bread of Life.

Instead of years going by with no eternal value to show for it.

Me and Jaylah (14 years old) have been in this Feed below daily for 8 years now, weaving the Word of His power into Her vocabulary as the Lord continues to light Her candle (spirit) with Spiritual understanding.

As of November 2021

Me and Jaylah have been in the Word for approximately 8 years now. She has been through the full,

Psalms 119	-	96 times (1 prayer a day)
Psalms	-	16 times (1 a day)
Proverbs	-	96 times (1 a day)
Gospels	-	96 times (1 chapter a day) (rotating all 4 Gospels)
The Letters	–	(2 years now - 1 chapter a day) All in about 1 hour a day.

Pro. 8
A wise man discerns both time and judgment.

I have done much discerning with time and judgment over the years by making the right decisions (executing judgment), to keep their Spiritual feed through the day, every day! Hardest thing I have ever done, but worth it all, for that forever Stuff. This kind of Spiritual feed provides more than enough "substance of Faith" to fatten up the inner Man (Christ in Her; Her hope of glory) over the outer man, causing the outer man to pine away with its dominance, while the inner Man flourishes rich and strong.

It is not as hard as you might think; there is a lot of wasted time in the Children's lives that just passes you by! Making the right decisions (for the Feed must go on), chasing their Feed against the clock, and making the holy decisions required to keep the Feed. In other words, discerning both time and judgment (right decisions).

Faithfully and daily as much as possible without discouraging Her or squashing Her childhood. But rather in the nurture and admonition of the Lord, weaving the Word in all Our activities,

The only Food available for the inner Man (Eternal life) is the Bread and Water of Life, and nothing else!

(See my book "God's Peculiar Treasures" for more information on Children.)

The Spiritual Feed Of The Children

(see my book "God's Peculiar Treasures")

Then, Spiritual feeding of the Children is much more complicated than natural feed! Natural feed deals with the food they feed, and you're done with the outer man. But the Spiritual Feed deals with the soul and spirit by the Word (Spirit) of God, the unseen - inner Man. I try to keep My feed and the Children's feed every day as My covenant part of their eternal Promises! As I learned how to keep My daily Feed, I would also keep their daily Feed, which is guaranteed for 3 generations.

Feeding the little Lambs!

Every day, I have a sense of urgency concerning the children's Faith (Feed). Every day, I monitor the measure of their Faith, which needs to be ever-increasing in their innocent little lives.

Jn. 21
If you love Me, feed My little Lambs.

What eternal things are you doing for your New Creation (Child) of God?

1Jn. 2

Whosoever, does the will (Word) of God, lives forever!

And the "Whosoever" surely includes the Children!

1 Pt 1
Therefore, as newborn babes in Christ, desire the sincere Milk of the Word that you may grow.

Apostle Paul, writing to the adults in Churches, advised them to Feed on the Milk of God's word. As it is for all who begin in Christ Jesus (the Kingdom of God), They are to be nurtured in the Milk of God's word. How much more should your baby be Fed, as a New Creation of God, the Milk of His word! Both the young and old are to be Fed (Word) in Christ Jesus!

Pro. 12
A man's belly (spirit) shall be satisfied by the fruit (Word of God) of his mouth, and by the increase of his lips (daily Feeds) shall he be filled.

No fruit of the mouth (the Word) – no satisfaction – no increase of the lips – no filling – no planting - no harvest (of the Christ in You).

The child's soul and Spirit need to Spiritually feed on the Bread (Word) and Water (Holy Spirit) of Life!

It is not an option! This Feed should be paramount for the parents in securing the child's eternal future!

1Pt. 3
Let it not be the adorning of the outer man, but let it be the hidden Man of the heart.

Every parent cares for and feeds their child's body daily! But most parents do not Feed their child's soul and spirit daily, which is much more vital. I am sad to say that nine out of ten parents (even Christians) do not substantially Feed their Child's soul and spirit the Bread of Life, nor the Water of Life daily, as they do the child's body. In Mathew 19, even the Disciples tried to stop the children from going to Jesus (the Bread of Life).

Even these holy men of God could not see the Children's' need for the Bread of Life, nor could they see the potential of the Kingdom of God in the Children, and neither did I (as a Disciple), with my Child! Children are like little lambs: all they want is to be Led and Fed, not left to themselves (the outer man)!

Thank God I caught My granddaughter just in time. I started weaving the Word into her vocabulary at 4 years of age!

Blessed be the God and Father of My child, that has not checked my prayer to Him, nor His own love to Me.

The Children have been Spiritually neglected and abandoned for as long as they have been around.

Indeed, a grave tragedy!

It is this neglect and abandonment that has brought us to this state of man today. Children have always had a bad shake, always shuffled off and ignored!

Jer.2
Fainting for hunger (Bread of Life) at the top of every street!

Mt 18
And Jesus called a little child to Him and set him in the middle of them ,and said, truly I say to you, except you be converted, and become as little children, you shall not enter the Kingdom of Heaven.

Whoever, therefore, shall humble himself as a little child, the same is the greatest in the Kingdom of Heaven. And whoever receives one such little child in My name, receives Me.

But whosoever shall offend one of these little ones, which believe in Me, It would be better for him that a millstone tied to his neck, and drowned in the depth of the sea.

Biggest lie of the devil is that "the Children are too young!

There should be a wholesome and tenacious perspective of Life towards them, with a daily consciousness of the children' Interior as the source of their lives, rather than the exterior, for the Kingdom of God (their innocence) is within Them, As Jesus (God) has said!

The Spiritual feed will make or break your Child! For the window of the age of innocence is very narrow! The child's Innocence (3-4 years?) quickly disappears because of the dominance of the outer man and the influence of the world.

It is the parent's responsibility to maintain and retain the Child's innocence through the Holy Ghost through the Word of Life.

This is the time to redeem the Child's Spiritual inheritance through the "Regeneration of washing" (His word) of their soul and body through the Word of His power. This time frame (life map) of their early years is extremely crucial to their "hidden Man of the heart". Having the Child become familiar with their

Spiritual inheritance and weaving the Word of God into their vocabulary will provide a sure foundation for their Heavenly identification and their Spiritual riches in Christ Jesus and Life everlasting.

As parents, we need to safeguard our Inner Man before it gets swallowed up by the world and the flesh. Parents are responsible for the feeding of the Child's soul and will be held accountable! The Milk, Bread, and Meat of God's word will keep the Child's life safe from eternal death, their feet from falling, and their eyes from tears; so that they may Live and be ever so mindful of God in the sunshine of Life!

Lam. 2
So, I cry out in the night: in the beginning of the watches, I pour out My heart like water before the face of the Lord: I lift up My hands toward Him for the Life of the young children that faint for hunger (the Bread of Life) at the top of every street.

Jeremiah was able to see these spiritual skeletons of the Children: can you? It is one thing to neglect your inward Man, but neglecting the Children's hidden Man of the heart – God's peculiar treasure, is totally unacceptable and Spiritual suicide for all involved! It shocks my mind how I could go on for so long (as a mature Christian) without the Spiritual feed of the Child! How could I not see the desperate need to Spiritually feed them the Bread of Life?

Their little brains are like sponges, and their little Hearts are like blank tapes, open to hear and ready to receive. They only need to hear and see (good Words and good works), until they can understand. When it comes to Faith, it's only a matter of hearing for them each time!

Starting right away, the "doing part" for them will come later, as their inner Man matures and takes control over the outer man.

Faith comes by hearing and hearing by the Word of God! Therefore, the hearing of the Word should be monumental in their lives! Always have some hearing going on, to put Faith in Them. It is a tragedy for a Child to reach the age of 7 without hearing (Feeding) the Word of the Kingdom. This hearing of the Word must be a constant in their Life!

Ps. 119
I would of perished in my affliction (ignorance) unless the Law of the Lord had been my delight.

Do not waste Their time because the Devil is already planning his ungodly agenda (Feed) for your Child right now, which does not include eternal life.

So, get busy, for the "Wise discerns both time and judgment", but a fool does not.
and a good man walks in his integrity, and his Children are blessed after him.

The Children's Bread!

Eternal Confessions for the Little Lambs

(Pre-prayer for each sitting)

Ps. 45
My heart is stirred by a royal theme (Our inheritance) as I speak my verses to my King (Christ in Me).

Pro. 18
The Words in my mouth are as deep waters and the wellspring of Wisdom as a flowing brook.

Pro. 18
My belly (spirit) shall be satisfied by the fruit (words) of my mouth, and by the increase of my lips, I shall be filled. For the power of Life and death is in my Tongue (tamed).

Psalm 119

1 prayer a day (breakfast or supper) – crucial! The 1st prayer on the 1st day.

The 2nd prayer on the 2nd day - etc.

Have the Child confess the Hebrew alphabet to figure out what letter the day is. Then, have them confess the sign and the meanings of the letter of that day. Then, have them confess the 8 verses of prayer.

א ALEF – the 1st

Numeric Value (1)

Ancient

Sign   =   Ox-Head

Meanings   =   lead - strength – power

1
I AM blessed: as the undefiled in the Way, I walk in the Law of the Lord.

2
I AM: blessed: I keep His Word (revelations) and seek Him with My whole heart,

3
I also do no iniquity: I walk in His ways.

4
You have commanded Me to keep Your word (precepts – Divine nature) all the time.

5

Oh, that My ways were made to keep Your word (statues- Divine duties).

6

Then shall I not be ashamed when I have respect unto all Your commandments.

7

I will praise You with uprightness of heart as I learn the judgments (Our inheritance) of Your righteousness.

8

I will keep Your Word (statutes – Divine duties); do not utterly forsake Me.

The Voice of the Lord

Jn. 10
I AM: The Lord's sheep. I hear, know, and obey His voice, But the voice of a Stranger I will not follow!

Isa.50
Morning by morning He opens My ears to hear, as the Learned.

My Heavenly Father has given Me eyes to see Him - ears to hear Him, and a new heart to do His will – with a tamed tongue, for the power of life and death is in My tongue! (right now).

The Word of God

Jn. 1:1
In the beginning was the Word, and the Word was with God, and the Word is God.

Jn 1:12
And the Word became flesh and is now living in Me.

Rev. 19
He is dressed in clothes dipped in Blood, and His name is called the Word of God. The Word of life in Me is alive, quick, and powerful.

1 Jn. 1
That which was from the beginning, which We have heard, We have seen with our eyes, which We have looked upon and Our hands have touched, of the Word of Life.

Ps. 19
The Word of His power in Me is perfect, making me like Jesus.
The Word of His power in Me is sure, making me Wise.
The Word of His power in Me is right, rejoicing my heart.
The Word of His power in Me is pure, enlightening my eyes.

The Word of the Lord in Me is clean enduring (endearing) forever.
All the judgments of the Lord in Me are true and righteous.
More to be prized than gold, than plenty of rare gold:
sweeter also more than the honeycomb:

By them I AM: warned, and in keeping them there is a great reward.

Pro. 6
When I go, the Word will lead Me, When I sleep, the Word will keep Me,
When I awake, the Word will speak to Me.

1 Pt 1
I AM: Born again by the Word of God which lives in Me forever.

The Bride of Christ

Rm.7
I AM: a bride of Christ, married to the Lord!

Isa 54
My Maker is my Husband. His name is Jesus, my Savior, the Holy One of Israel.

1 Pt: 1
I AM: Holy because He is holy! He is the Vine, and I AM: one of the branches.

2 Cor.7
I AM: Perfecting holiness in the fear of God.

Eph 3
I always keep My thoughts and feelings on things Above, where Jesus is.

Pro. 14
My fear of the Lord is a fountain of Life.

Rm. 5
The love of God is poured in my heart by the Holy Ghost.

"I AM THAT I AM"

My inheritance in Christ Jesus: in Me: Part a

I AM:

Bought – crucified – baptized – born again - circumcised –

New creation – righteousness – free – I AM: a temple of the Lord.

My inheritance in Christ Jesus: in Me: Part b

I AM:

Called – sanctified – child – anointed – saint – servant – steward

Ambassador – priesthood – royal-hood – glorified - I AM: complete in Him.

My inheritance in Christ Jesus:, in Me: Part c

I AM:

Dead (and my Life is hid with God) – divine nature - branch – holding forth – laying hands –

Casting out devils – baptizing with the Holy Ghost – committed - pressing in –prisoner of the Lord - Christ in Me, My hope of glory.

The Blood of Jesus

1 Jn. 1:9

Jesus is My Lamb of God, who takes away the sin of the world!
The Blood of Jesus is My super Soap! It washes Me white as snow.
His blood washes Me from anything - anywhere – anytime - forever!

Eph. 4:32

I AM: Kind, tender hearted, forgiving, and ready for every good work.

Pro. 11:25

My liberal soul shall be made fat: for He who waters shall Himself be watered.

2 Tim. 1:7

I DO NOT HAVE THE SPIRIT OF FEAR!
I DO NOT HAVE THE SPIRIT OF THIS WORLD!
BUT I HAVE THE SPIRIT OF GOD!

Rm. 8:11

I HAVE THE SAME SPIRIT THAT RAISED JESUS FROM THE DEAD,
THE SPIRIT OF POWER, LOVE AND A SOUND MIND. (Somewhere in Me)

Jn. 14:26

The Holy Spirit is teaching Me all about Jesus, My neighbor, and the Kingdom of God.

Ps. 118:17

Therefore, I will not die, but live. God, My Father, will raise Me up from the dead.

The New Birth

1 Pt 1:23

I AM:
Born again by the Word of God which lives in Me forever.

2 Cor. 5:17

I AM:
A new Creation in Christ, old things are passed away,
all things have become new, all things are of God.

Jer. 15

I AM:

Called by His name, therefore, as He is, so I AM: in this world. (1 Jn. 4).

1 Thess. 2

I will walk worthy of God,
He has called Me to His glory and to His heaven.

Ps.139

I will praise You, O Lord, for I AM: fearfully and wonderfully made.

Pro. 10

Therefore, My mouth brings forth Wisdom, and My tongue talks of judgment!

And these are the judgments of the Lord:

I AM: the Saved   -   not the lost,

I AM: the Righteous   -   not a sinner,

I AM: the Healed   -   not the sick,

I AM: the Wise   -   not the fool,

I AM: the Rich   -   not the poor,

I AM: a Giver   -   not a taker,

I AM: the Top   -   not the bottom,

I AM: the Head   -   not the tail.

ONLY IN CHRIST JESUS!

The Mouth

A

My mouth is like the mouth of God   -   My words are Spirit and Life   -   My lip of truth is forever.

The power of Life and death is in my tongue (Pro. 18).

B

My mouth is a wellspring of Wisdom   -   I AM: enriched in all knowledge and speech

My answer is always from Lord   -   My mouth is a well of Life   -   My lip of Truth will feed many

C

My tongue is a tree of Life   -   My belly is satisfied by my words   -   Milk and honey under My tongue

My soft answer turns away anger   -   My wise tongue heals   -   preserves   —   and protects.

D

Many words sin   -   Words in My mouth like deep waters   -   By my words justified or condemned

Words pierce like a sword and can break the bone.

Jn. 6:63

THE WORD OF HIS POWER IN MY MOUTH IS SPIRIT AND LIFE.

Ps. 45:1

My tongue is the pen of God, writing the Words of Life on the paper of My heart!

Pro. 31

The law of kindness is always on My tongue.

Ps. 19:14

*Let all the Words of My mouth, and the thoughts (feelings) of My heart,
be always beautiful for You, and My neighbor.*

Jer.15:19

*If, I take away the vile (crooked) from the Precious (Christ in You),
then,
my mouth will be as the mouth of God.*

The Fear of God in Me

Ps. 103:17

*The mercy of the Lord is upon Me from everlasting to everlasting,
and His righteousness to Our children's children, because I do fear Him.*

Pro. 14:27

My fear of God is a Fountain of Life, taking Me away from the snares of death.

Jer. 32:40

God has put His spirit of fear into My heart so that I will not depart from Him.

Gal. 4:6

Even, the Spirit of His son into My heart, crying "Abba Father".

Isa. 11: 3

Therefore, I have a quick Understanding in the fear of the Lord.

1 Pt. 1:16

I AM: HOLY; FOR GOD IS HOLY.
(My Spirit is most holy - God's residence day and night - New Heart - Born again.)

Phil. 2:12

I AM: working out My own salvation with fear and trembling.

Pro. 14:19

The evil must bow before the Good and the wicked at the gates of the Righteous.

1 Cor. 7:1

I AM: Perfecting holiness in the fear of God.

Ps. 12.6:3

The rod of the wicked shall not rest upon the Land of the Righteous (the Christ in You),
except They put forth Their hands unto iniquity. (And I will not!)

Chapter 10

The "Circumcision of Christ"

Col. 2: 11
In Whom you also are circumcised, with the circumcision made without hands, in the putting off the body the sins of the flesh by the Circumcision of Christ: Buried with Him in baptism, wherein you are also risen with Him, through the faith of the operation of God, as He raised Him from the dead.

Our Heavenly Father (even though not seen) did not create us and save us just to leave us on our own to fend for ourselves.

He has made full provision for the body, soul, and spirit because of a lifetime association with the flesh and the world system, as opposed to a brief time in the Spirit.

So, because we have this Treasure (Christ in You) in earthen vessels (flesh) and a jealous Adversary (the Devil and his bunch of the Father's love for us) that is stronger and invisible, the Father has leveled the playing field (Salvation) by fully equipping us for the perfection of the Body of Christ, and life everlasting. We are buried with Him in baptism and risen with Him through Faith (believing) in the operation of God (Circumcision of Christ) in the "putting off the body the sins of the flesh." Jesus has provided an inheritance (Circumcision of Christ) for us in the putting off of the sins of the flesh by His holy, perfect life. If we can believe (by habit of believing) this operation of God, we can be free of the sins of the flesh!

Rm 8
For the Law (the Word) of the Spirit of Life in Christ Jesus has set us free from the law of sin and death.

So, it is necessary to make your work fit for the outside (Fasting - holy flesh). When you shut down the flesh by Fasting, you shut down the old man and the Devil, thus leveling the playing Field! God has made provision for the Interior (Christ in You) and the exterior (holy flesh) by the "Circumcision of Christ" which comes through Faith and Fasting (holy flesh). Most Christians concentrate only on the interior and neglect the exterior because it is more work (Faith).

Provision for the new Creation – body, soul, and spirit:

For the body – the "Circumcision of Christ"

For the soul – The Word of His power (the Mind of Christ)

For the spirit – the Holy Spirit (New Heart)

The Holy Spirit needs holy flesh to produce holy Fruit and to express Himself and the power of God that keeps us.

How could we live a holy life without holy flesh? By Faith in the "Circumcision of Christ," by Faith (Fasting), that's how!

Your Spiritual inheritance kicks in much faster with holy flesh (fasting) – the Circumcision of Christ.

It is a Circumcision (already cut away by Jesus) of the flesh made without hands. He did it without your help. Jesus conquered the flesh and has now made provision for the flesh of the Saints through believing (Fasting) in the Circumcision of Christ!

Rm. 8
Sin shall not have dominion over you!

Some examples of a physical Circumcision of Christ.

After about a dozen Fasts or so, I started having victory over my flesh, from all the many "No's." Having knowledge and Faith in the Circumcision of Christ (Jesus's provision for the flesh in the putting off of the body sin) and integrity to Fast (New Wineskin) set me free from the law of sin and death.

For example:

Before I was saved, as a young man, I was a sexually active person. When my sex organ was stimulated, I had no power to stop it, which would eventually lead me to sin. But Jesus' victory over all sin (the understanding of the Circumcision of Christ) is transferred to me as a believer by Faith (confessing and acting like you're free - by calling things that be not as though they are - until the Word of His power kicks in and takes over), co-laboring together with God in God's operation made in me without hands, for the putting off the body the sins of the flesh. The power comes through the understanding and Faith in the doctrine (teaching) of the Circumcision of Christ.

Pro. 24
A Wise man is strong, and a man of understanding increases strength.

1 Pt. 4:1
For as much then as Christ has suffered for us in the flesh, arm yourselves likewise with the same mind: for he that has suffered in the (holy) flesh has ceased from sin.

My sex organ does not get stimulated (hard) anymore because of my Faith in putting off of the body the sins of the flesh. The warfare of the flesh has gone from the physical to the mental – from feelings to thoughts (of the Mind (Words) of Christ) - from the carnal to the Divine, which is much easier to squash! This is because of the Circumcision of Christ, which levels up the playing field. Masturbation used to rob me of my Spiritual inheritance (victory, etc.) until the Circumcision of Christ quickened me into the righteousness (freedom) of God.

Col. 2
And you, being dead in your sins and the uncircumcision (unclean blood - belly - body) of your flesh, has He quickened you together with Him, having forgiven you of all your trespasses?

"Dead in the uncircumcision of your flesh": in the passing of the holy flesh: in the rejoicing to do evil: in the wasting away: in the ignoring of Zion (Body of Christ – the Church): in the ignoring of Fasting (holy blood and body), and in the coziness of your disposition with the will of God for your life. Can you remember your early days of Salvation, your honeymoon with the Lord, in the days of the gladness of your heart, when you would do anything for Jesus!

After I was saved, I could not listen (the Circumcision of Christ) to the radio with its worldly messages anymore, which spoke nothing of Jesus and His kingdom. Even the songs that I had grown up with all my life, that were dear to my heart, now had a sour taste because none of it was going up to God. Any kind of conversation without Christ was just futile to me in the days of the gladness (Salvation) of my heart. This is because of God's divine nature that is now in me - a new heart - even the Circumcision of Christ.

Duet.30
The Lord your God will circumcise your heart and the hearts of your children.
[He will remove the desire to sin from your heart],

So that you may love the Lord your God with all your heart and all your soul, so that you may live (as a recipient of His blessings).

Removing the desire to sin!

God gives us a whole salvation (body, soul, and spirit) with its provisions. We need to receive this Circumcision of Christ by Faith for it to work in our lives. As a matter of fact, God rolled away all the reproach (unbelief) of Israel (Joshua 5) by just a natural circumcision of the flesh, giving them a new clean slate – how much more shall the Circumcision of Christ purge your consciousness from dead works to serve the living God.

Spiritual Circumcision of Christ.

Heb. 9:13-14
If the blood of bulls and goats and the ashes of a heifer sprinkling the unclean, sanctifies to the purifying of the flesh, how much more shall the Blood of Christ, Who through the eternal Spirit offered Himself without spot to God, purge your conscious (thoughts and memories) from dead works, to serve the living God.

Purge your conscious (mind) from dead works! When a person gets genuinely born again and receives the Blood of God, it cuts away all the memory ties to their old nature (crooked man) that used to lead them so that they may freely serve the Father as a Servant of God with the mind of Christ, which is your crown of life. (Do not lose it!)

2 Cor.5
Therefore, if any man is in Christ, he is a New Creature; old things (all) are passed - away.
All things have become new, and all things are of God, joined unto the Lord in one (Holy) Spirit.

In the new Creation – Christ in You, old things are passed away runs right down to the DNA.

This is God's provision for the holy flesh to accommodate the Holy Spirit so that we may bear the holy Fruits of the Holy Spirit in us. If you take the carnal flesh out of the equation, the Devil has nothing to work with, for most of his onslaught comes in through the carnal flesh (carnal mind). Shutting down the flesh by Fasting shuts down the Battlefield! The goal is to maintain the holy flesh, which constantly condemns sin, fueling confidence in yourself and the power of God so that you can execute the judgments of the Lord in your life, here and now.

When a Christian truly suffers (Fasting and suffering for His namesake) to resolve his Spiritual life uprightly with a whole heart (body, soul, and mind), then the Christ in You will immediately quicken you into the victories of the Lord.!

Rm. 8:3
For what the law could not do, in that it was weak in the flesh,
God sending His own Son in the likeness of sinful flesh,
and for sin, condemned sin in the (holy) flesh.

Jesus condemned sin in His holy flesh, and so should you! Paul realized
the importance of the holy flesh and purposed to keep it.

1 Cor. 9
Therefore, I run in such a way, as not without aim; I box in a way, as not beating the air, but I discipline my body and make it my slave (Fast - holy flesh), so that after I have preached to others, so that I, myself will not be disqualified.

Jer. 11
Therefore, I will not let the holy flesh pass from me.

Having the power of God does not exclude You from the holy flesh. Paul could be disqualified without it, for it is the Law of the House! Pride (serving the Lord in the comforts of your own flesh and the world) is a transgression against God. We need to let the Lord be in control of our mouths (food) and tongues (words) through Fasting; the body and soul will follow. The power of God must be safeguarded on a Tamed tongue, lest you get mad and hurt somebody. God purges the mouth and the tongue through the refining fires of Fasting, consecrating them to His will. Once You have the belly (Fasting) in control, then You can start on the Fasting of the tongue (words).

Jer. 15
If you take away the vile from the precious, then shall your mouth be as My mouth.

We need to focus on the root (holy flesh) of the tree, not all the little leaves at the top. The holy flesh is like a radar for sin and any incoming undesirables, both in the body and the soul. Fasting is critical for obtaining the holy flesh and keeping it, which is the foundation on which God will build Your inheritance (Christ in You). The term holy flesh is not mentioned much, but it is in many other ways. It is a doctrine for the Wise that only comes through Fasting.

(Some "holy flesh" Scriptures are below.)

S.O.S 5
I have put off my coat (flesh); how then shall I put it on again? I have washed my feet; how then shall I defile them?

Rm. 8
The Law of the Spirit of Life in Christ Jesus has set me free from the law of sin and death.

S.O.S 7

My waist is as a golden chalice that never lacks blended Wine (Holy Ghost).

And many more like these all over the Place, pointing to holy flesh.

The enemy desires to rob us of this holy flesh right from the beginning. He knows that if he can get control of the mouth (food) and the tongue (words), the blood and body will soon follow. Prayer flows freely in the Circumcision of Christ (Fasting – holy flesh), for the flesh is holy during the Fast - the soul is arrested by the Word - and the spirit is Spirit (the same Spirit that raised Jesus from the dead), with a readiness to avenge all disobedience.

When in a Fast, the purity (Spiritual Inheritance) of your spirit (Spirit) quickly flows out of the heart, over into your soul, which flows over into the body, creating an atmosphere for meditation that is conducive to the Bread of His presence (Holy Spirit), generating a deep Spiritual feed, which outweighs any other kind of feed that the world or the Devil would try to bribe you with.

Ps. 9:1
I will praise You, oh Lord with a whole heart (Fasting - holy blood – holy soul – holy spirit).

Meditations:

For the "Christ in You – Your hope of (God's) glory" to feed on!

The Bread of Life is soul food.

Ps. 104
My meditation of Him will be sweet: I will be glad in the Lord.

Meditation of the Word is prophetic: You prophesy to your Spirit (inward Man), in righteousness and true holiness, the communication of Your faith firing up every good thing in You, in Christ.

As a king (queen), reigning on Your throne of judgment (the will) over Your soul and body, scattering all evil with Your eyes, as a Stranger in the earth, looking for that City (the Christ in You) whose Maker and foundations are God.

With the Word of His power being fitted for the lips as a precious jewel. Your mouth is a well of Life pouring out the mysteries of God. Your tongue as the pen of God, writing the Words of Life on the hearts of the children of men, as a true Scribe of the Lord!

Ps. 45
My heart is stirred by a royal theme as I recite My verses to my King.

The Wisdom that comes through this kind of meditation (full course Feeding) is Spiritual, not earthly! It is between the lines, from the Holy Ghost!

Pro. 12
He who tills (meditates) his land shall have abundant food (Wisdom), but he who chases fantasies lacks judgment.

Meditation exceeds reading, like light exceeds darkness.

Reading is superficial, meditating is super spiritual.

Reading is natural (the exterior), meditating is divine (the Interior).

Crying note: Children should be taught this meditation (Their Inheritance) as soon as They can speak during their life map! Lay God's foundation in Them!

"I AM THAT I AM"

(This is My Spiritual inheritance bought with the Blood of Jesus. It cannot be earned. It can only be received by Faith!)

Theme

Hebs.7:28
The Word of the Oath (Bible), which was since the Law, makes the Son (Daughter - Me) forever.

Eph. 4:24

I AM: putting on the New Man, which after God is made in Righteousness and true Holiness.

Ps. 45:1
With My tongue as Pen of God - writing the Law of the Lord on the tablet of My heart (Pro. 7:3).

My heart is stirred (Holy Ghost) by a royal Theme (My inheritance) as I recite my verses (the Word) to my King. (For as He is, so I AM in this world. 1 Jn. 4:17).

Introduction

I (selah) AM (selah):

I AM: Bought with the Blood of Jesus. My body and soul belong to God. Rm. 8:11

I AM: Crucified: with Christ: nevertheless, I live: not me, but Christ that lives in Me. Gal. 2:20

I AM: Baptized: buried with Jesus in baptism – and risen with Him through the faith of the operation of God. Col. 2:12

I AM: Born Again: by the incorruptible Word (Seed) of God. 1 Pt 1:23

I AM: Circumcised: (New heart): done without hands! In the putting off of the body, the sins of the flesh. Col. 2:11

I AM: New Creation: in Christ, old things are passed away, all things are new; all things are of God. 2 Cor. 5:17

I AM Righteousness: of God in Christ Jesus, through the "perfect law of liberty." Rm. 3:21

I AM: Free: for the Law of the Spirit of Life in Christ Jesus has set me free from the law of sin and death. Rm. 8:2

1 Cor. 6:19
I AM: Temple of the Holy Ghost: fearfully and wonderfully Made.

I WILL NOT DIE BUT LIVE (FOREVER)! GOD WILL RAISE ME UP FROM THE DEAD.

Content

I AM: Called: to be in this world as Jesus is in this world. Rm. 1:6 1 Jn. 2:6

I AM: Sanctified: set apart, to be humble, and holy, clothed in praise. Rm. 8:30

I AM: Holy: because He is holy. He is the Vine, and I Am one of the Branches.

I AM: Child: of God. Jesus is My Brother, and He is not ashamed of it! Gal. 4:6

I AM: Anointed: and appointed to do the will of God. I will live forever.1 Jn.1:2

I AM: Saint: of God; not because of my works; but because of the Blood of Jesus. 1 Cor. 1:2

I AM: Servant: of Christ; spiritually equipped for every and any need! 1 Cor. 4:1

I AM: Ambassador: of Jesus Christ for the work of the Kingdom of God. 2 Cor. 5:20

I AM: Steward (Keeper): of the mysteries of God, which has been hidden for ages and generations, now made known to Me. 1 Cor. 4:1

I AM: Priesthood: in Christ; I stand before the God of Israel for the people! 1 Pt. 2:9

I AM: Royalty: in Christ Jesus. Ps.148:4-5 1 Cor. 4:8. Ps. 47:9 Rev.1:8

Summary

I AM: Dead (old nature): and My life is hidden with Christ in God. Col. 3:3

I AM: In God's divine nature: with the same Spirit that raised Jesus from the dead. 2 Pt.1:3

I AM: Branch: and Jesus is the Vine; in labors of love; bearing fruit unto good works. Jn. 15:5

I AM: Holding forth: the Word of His power with boldness and authority. Phil. 2:16

I AM: LAYING HANDS: on the sick in humility with many tears (by Faith)! Mk. 16:17

I AM: CASTING OUT: devils with the love of God in the Name of Jesus (by Faith)! Mk.16:17

I AM: BAPTIZING: the children of men in the Holy Ghost (by Faith)! Mt. 28:19

I AM: Glorified: in Christ Jesus. Rom. 8

I AM: Pressing in: towards the mark of the high calling of God in Christ Jesus. Phil. 3:14

I AM: Committed: to the Word of His grace; building Me up and giving Me an inheritance in Christ. Acts 20:32

I AM: Prisoner: of the Word of God, and a defender of the Faith. Eph. 3:1

I AM: by Him as one brought up with Him.

I AM: His delight daily, rejoicing always before the Lord! Pro. 8:30

Col. 1: 26-27
Even the Mystery (the Word of His power) that has been hidden for generations and generations, but is now known to the Church (Me) that is,

CHRIST IN YOU (ME) - THE (MY) HOPE OF GLORY!

Eph. 5: 1
Be you therefore imitators of God, as dearly loved children!

Phil. 2:5
So, let this mind be in You, that was also in Christ Jesus, who in the form of God thought it not robbery to be equal with God: but made himself of no reputation, and took upon him the form of a servant . . .

Philemon 1:6
That the communication (operation) of your Faith (inheritance) may become effective by the acknowledging (with your mouth) of every good thing in You, in Christ.

Cor. 2:16
I have the mind (Words) of Christ (which is My crown of Life)!

I will always wear My crown of Life. (Lam. 5:16)

1 Pt. 3:3-4
Let not the adorning be that of the outward man, the braiding of hair, and the wearing of gold, or the putting on of apparel: But let it be the "hidden Man (Christ) of the heart," in that which is not corruptible, even the ornament of a meek and quiet spirit, which in the sight of God is of great price.

P.S.

Mt. 11: 11
Truly, I say to you, among those born of women, there has not risen anyone greater than John the Baptist, yet the One who is least in the kingdom of God is greater than he.

Col.1: 27
Christ in Me – My hope of (God's) glory!

ZION – Meditation #4 – Kings and Queens of the Earth

(A true king-queen is anyone who rules from the throne of Their heart, over Their soul and body, in Truth.)

Philemon 1:6
That the communication (operation) of your Faith (inheritance) may become effective
by acknowledging (with your mouth) every good thing in You, in Christ.

Theme

Rev. 1:5-6

From Jesus Christ, who is the faithful witness, and the first begotten from the dead,
and the Prince of the kings (holy Christians) of the earth.

To Him that loved us and washed us from our sins with His own blood,
and has made Us kings and priests to God and his Father,
to Him be glory and dominion forever and ever.

Rm. 5:17

So, if by one man's offence, death reigned by one; how much more
They (Whosoever will believe) that receive abundance of grace, and
the gift of Righteousness, will reign in life by One, Jesus Christ.

I (selah) AM (selah):
Reigning in life by the Christ in Me - My hope of glory!

Introduction

Gal. 2:20

I (selah) AM (selah):
Crucified with Christ, nevertheless I live,
not I,
but the Christ that lives within Me.

The life I live in this body, I now live by the Faith (Kingship) of the Son of God who loved Me,
and gave Himself for Me (and has made Us kings - queens and priests to God and his Father).

Content

Ps. 47:9
The princes (Christians) of the peoples, are gathered-together, even the
People (Church - Body of Christ) of the God of Abraham (Father of Faith),
for the Shields of the earth belong to God.

Ps. 113:7

For He raises up the poor from the dust, and lifts the poor and needy out of the dunghill.
That He may set him - her with princes (princesses), even the princes of His people.

Rev. 1:5

Jesus Christ, the Prince of the kings – queens (the holy ones of Israel - the Church)
of the earth. (God being the King of kings).

Ps. 45:7

You love righteousness and hate wickedness: therefore, God, Your God,
has anointed You above all Your fellow-kings-queens (saints).

Pro. 29:4

Therefore, I, as king - queen (over My soul and body) establish my land (Christ in Me)
by judgment! (I AM: always discerning, both time and judgment for the glory of God.)

Ps. 144:10

For it is He (Jesus) that gives salvation unto kings – queens, and delivers
David (the Church – Body of Christ) from the hurtful sword.

Ps. 68:29

Because of Your temple at Jerusalem shall kings (Christian saints) bring
gifts (vows of holiness and sacrifices of praise and thanksgiving) unto You.

Ps. 138:4-5

All the kings - queens of the earth shall praise You, O Lord, when They hear the
Words (Gospel) of Your mouth. They shall sing in the ways (Gospel) of the Lord:
for great is the glory of the Lord.

1 Cor. 4:8

Now are you full, now are you rich.
You have reigned as kings-queens without us (the Apostles).

Gospels

Fear not little Flock, for it is the Father's good pleasure to give you the kingdom.

2 Chron. 16:9

The eyes of the Lord run back and forth throughout the earth,
looking for Whom (Whomsoever will - Me) He may show Himself strong.

Ps. 60

The Sons of Strangers (Christians) shall build up Your walls,
and their kings-queens will minister unto You.

Rev. 1:6

The Lord has made Us kings (queens) and priests unto Our God!

Ps. 80:17

Let Your hand be upon the Man of Your right hand (Me and You), even the son of man (whomsoever will) which you have made strong for Yourself.

Ps. 102:16

The Eternal builds up Zion, appearing in His majesty, He turns to the Forlorn (Christians in Spiritual warfare), despising not their prayer.

Job 22:28

Therefore, I shall also decree a thing and it shall be established unto Me.

Ps. 45:15

With gladness and rejoicing shall They (the Body of Christ) be brought: They shall enter the King's palace (Heaven).

Ps. 132::18

Our enemies will be clothed with shame, but Our crown (Mind of Christ) will flourish.

Lam. 5:16 - 1 Cor. 2:16

I will always wear My crown of life, even the mind of Christ.

Summary

Ps. 45:16

Instead of your fathers will be your Children, whom the Lord will make princes (princesses) in all the earth

Ps. 132

If Your children will keep My covenant and My testimony that I will teach Them, then, Their children will also sit upon Your throne.

Ps. 47

For He raises up the poor (the Spiritual dead) from the dust (flesh), and lifts the Poor (in flesh- holy) and Needy (of Jesus) out of the dunghill (world), that He may set them with princes, even the princes-princesses of His people (The Body of Christ).

1 Pt.2:9

For You are a royal priesthood, a holy nation, a chosen generation (all by the Blood of Jesus).

P.S.

Ecc. 4:14

In a rebellion (a life without God) a young man (women) may rise to the throne (Christ in You), even though he was born poor (no Knowledge of God) within the Realm (Body of Christ).

ZION - Meditation #3 – The Bride of Christ

The "Content" section of this med is to be roasted (memorized) and swallowed (meditated) as the precious Substance (Christ in You) of the diligent.

NOT JUST READ.

(Which is far better than aimless, wandering thoughts, looking unto the ends of the earth, that are never satisfied.)

Pro. 12
A lazy man does not roast that which he took in the hunt (the Word): but the Substance (Christ in You – Your hope of glory) of the diligent is precious.

Theme

Ps. 45:10-16
Hearken, oh Daughter (Zion - the Church – the Christian – Me – and "Whomsoever will"), and consider, and incline thine ear. Forget your own people, and your father's house (their earthly thinking). Then shall the King (Jesus) greatly desire thy beauty.
(The Christ in You – the hope of glory!)

For He is your Lord; You worship him.
The Daughter of Tyre (Gentiles) shall be there with a Gift (Faith);
Even the rich (Saved) among the people shall intreat (pray) thy favour.

The King's daughter (Zion - the Church - Me) is all glorious within
(Christ in Me – My hope of glory!)

Her clothing is of made gold (Wisdom). She shall be brought unto the king in a dazzling wedding dress (Holy Ghost) of needlework (fulfilled testing's of God)).

The Virgins (holy-overcomers), Her companions that follow Her (Zion), shall be brought unto thee. With gladness and rejoicing shall they be brought:
They shall enter into the King's palace.

Ps. 50:1-2

Out of Zion (The Body of Christ – the Christian), the perfection of beauty, (so peerless), God has shined forth (the God of gods is flashing)!

Introduction

Rev. 9:10

Come, and I will show you the Wife (Body of Christ - Church - Me) of the Lamb!

Rm. 7:4
(To the whole Church)

*(Its) You, my brethren, that are dead to the law (of sin and death) by the Body of Christ,
that You should be married to Another, even unto Him that has been raised from the dead,
that You should bring forth Fruit (of Spirit) unto God.*

Isa. 54:5

*Your Maker is your Husband; the Lord of Hosts (angelic armies) is His name;
and your Redeemer is the Holy One of Israel.*

S.O.S. 1:4

The King has brought Me into His chamber (Zion - the Body of Christ – the Church).

1 Cor. 6:17

*I (selah) AM (Selah):
Now joined to the Lord in one (Holy) Spirit!*

Rev. 22:17

For the Spirit and the Bride (Me) say, "Come, Lord Jesus, come."

Jm. 1:23 (The Message)

*Do not fool yourself into thinking you are a hearer of the Word, when you are anything but,
letting the Word go in one ear and out the other. Act (be) what you hear!*

*Those who hear and do not act are like those who look in the mirror, and walk away,
And soon after have no idea of who they are or what they look like.*

*But Whoever catches a glimpse of Himself (the Christ in You – Your hope of glory), in the Mirror
of God's Word shall be blessed in all His deeds ("as He is, so are We in this world"). (1 Jn. 4: 17)*

*(Do you think I see my outer self when I look in the Mirror (word) of God. No!
I always see the Christ in Me – My hope of glory!*

Everything I hear, say, and do, is from the "high place" of Christ in Me – My hope of glory!)

Content

(Song of Solomon or The Song of Songs)

Philemon 1:6

*That the communication (operation) of your Faith (inheritance) may become effective
by the acknowledging (with your mouth) of every good thing in You, in Christ.*

Groom (Jesus)
(My Beloved speaking to the Christ in Me says,)

*"Who is this glowing like the dawn, fair as the moon, clear as the sun,
ravishing as the night sky with its galaxies of stars." (6:10) - the Message*

Bride (the Christ in Us)

My hair is a royal tapestry, the King is held captive by its braids. (S.O.S 7:5 N.I.V.)

My head is like Mount Carmel (Crowned with the Mind of Christ and its manifold Wisdom of God) (7:5)

My eyes are as wells of Light deep with mystery. (Scattering all the evil that is before Me). (7:4 - the Message)

My nose is as the tower of Ivory. (Smelling any kind of flesh on the horizon.) (7;4. N.I.V)

My cheeks are radiant with rows of jewels - and My neck with chains of gold. (1:10)

My mouth is a well of Life (Pro. 10) (Flowing rivers of Living waters.).

Groom

"You have ravished My heart, My sister My spouse, with one of Your eyes: with one chain of Your neck". (4:9)

Bride

My tongue with its Law of kindness (Pro. 31) and the power of Life and death. (Pro.18).

My lips drop as the Honeycomb; Milk and Honey (the Word) are under My tongue. (5:3)

My Lip of Truth feeds many and will be established forever. (Pro. 10:21)

My teeth are like a flock of sheep that are shorn, that just come up from the washing. (6:5)

My neck is like the tower of David, built for war, whereon hang a thousand warriors, all mighty Men of war. (4:4) - That commands notice – all heads turn in awe and admiration. (I will not bend – bow – or burn.)

Groom

"You are fair My love; there is no spot in You. How beautiful (breathtaking) You are. How pleasing, oh my Love, with Your delights. (4:7)

There is no one like Her (the Christ in me) in the earth, never has been, never will be. She is a woman beyond compare (a new Creation - 2 Cor. 5:17).

My dove (Me - my spirit) is pure and innocent unto perfection." (6:8 - the Message)

Bride

My body is as a bundle of wheat (the Word) encircled by lilies. (7:2)

My waist is as a golden chalice that never lacks blended Wine (Holy Ghost).

My hands drop with myrrh, and My fingers with liquid myrrh (Pure true holiness). (5:5)

My graceful legs like jewels, the work of a Craftsman's hands. (7:1)

My feet are beautiful (Delivering the Gospel of Peace).

Groom

"As the Lily among thorns, so is My love among the daughters." (2:2)

Bride

I AM: a garden enclosed: and a spring shut up and a fountain sealed: (4:12) with all manner pleasant fruits, and all the chief spices.

I AM: a fountain of gardens, and a well of Living waters.

While the King sits at His table, My ointment (Essence of His presence) sends forth its sweet savor. (1:12)

His left hand is under My head, and His right hand around my waist! (2:6)

Groom

"Turn Your eyes away from Me, for they have overcome Me"! (6:5)

Bride

I sleep, but my heart is awake: it is the voice of My Beloved knocking, saying,

"Open to Me, My Sister, My Love (Body of Christ) My Dove, My Undefiled". (5:2)

Our Beloved put His hand by the hole of the door, and Our hearts started pounding at the thought of Him. (5:4)

Awake, North Wind; and come you south wind: blow upon My garden that the Spices thereof may flow out. (4:16)

I will let My Beloved come into His garden and eat His pleasant fruits (of the Spirit)."

2 Cor. 5
Therefore, If anyone is in Christ they are a new Creation. Old things are passed away, All things have become new, and all things are of God, Who has joined us to the Lord in one Spirit.

1 Pt. 3
So, let it not be the adorning of the outward man: the braiding of hair, and the wearing of gold or the putting on of apparel: But let it be the "hidden Man (Christ in You) of the heart," in that which is not corruptible, even the ornament of a meek and quiet spirit, which is in the sight of God of great price (Christ in You, the hope of glory).

Gen. 1
Let every Seed (Word) produce after its own kind! - "As He is, so are We in this world". (1Jn. 4)

Summary

Phil. 2:5

Let this mind be in You, that was also in Christ Jesus:
Who being in the form of God thought it not robbery
to be equal with God.

Eph.4:23-24

Therefore, I (selah) AM (Selah):
Being renewed in the spirit of My mind by putting on
the new Man (Christ in Me – My hope of glory), which is like God.

Ps.17:15

As for Me, I do behold Your face in righteousness.
I AM: awake, with Your likeness.

Ps. 11:7

The righteous Lord loves righteousness, and His countenance does behold the Upright (even Me).

Jer.31:22

The Lord has done a new thing in the earth.

A Woman with the strength of a Man (and a Man with the tenderness of a Women).

So then, I will reign from My heart, as a Son (king - queen),

from My body, as a virgin Daughter of Zion (in labors of Love},

and from My soul, as a Shield (Priesthood) of the earth,
ever living to make intercession!

Ps. 96:9

For strength and beauty are in His sanctuary!

Ps. 135
I (selah) AM (Selah):

God's Peculiar Treasure (in flesh - an earthen vessel)!

P.S.

Eph. 1

The Church (the Body of Christ – Zion - the Bride), the fullness of all,
that fills all in all, a world without end!

Chapter 11

The Mouth

TAMING THE TONGUE FOR THE BREAD OF LIFE!

THE MOUTH IS VITAL TO THE SPIRITUAL FEED OF THE CHILD.

THE PURER THE TONGUE, THE PURER THE LIFE.

Ecc. 6
All the labor of man is for his mouth, yet his appetite is not filled.

Most parents, even Christians, do not realize what a vital and dangerous role the mouth plays in a Child's life.

Physical and Spiritual success hinges on this rutter of God. Everything (and I do mean everything) a person does is for his mouth! They are either trying to fill their overcrowded belly or working to obtain the most they can, to glory in with their mouth, or the mouth is working to bring forth the good news and the high praises of God.

And without the tongue, a man's life would almost come to a halt.

The mouth of the outer man is never satisfied with food, and the tongue of the inner man is never satisfied with words (thoughts). This Scripture tells us that the mouth is a bottomless pit. James tells us that the tongue is an unruly member that no man can tame, setting ablaze the course of a man's life.

Pro. 12
Idle talk can pierce like a sword, but the Tongue of the Wise is healing.

Words can be very destructive, even dangerous unto death – as swords and razors cutting away at your life. We can see this activity of the mouth with a suicidal person and all the many negative persuasions of their mouth, both the mouth of the outer man and the mouth of the inner man.

Ps. 64
Who whet their tongue like a sword and bend their bows to shoot their arrows, even bitter words (even Christians at themselves).

Words can work in the positive as well. The words "I love you; will you marry me?" can quicken a woman's whole being to levels she had never known. In the case of someone becoming a doctor - how many times (in one way or another) would he have confessed his trade? And if he had stopped confessing it, he would not have made it, for the power of life and death is in the tongue, and they that love (tamed by Fasting) it will eat the fruit of it.

Pro. 23
"For as a man thinks in his heart, so is he."

Pro. 16

The heart of the Wise adds persuasiveness to his mouth and adds learning to his lips (and vice versa).

It is obvious from this verse that the mouth plays a major role in a Child's life. This can be seen in the natural, by the way, a child puts everything into their mouth, not any other part of the body, and also, in the spiritual, by all the many Scriptures in the mouth in the Bible - Proverbs - the Wisdom of God! (The Proverbs of God are full of Spiritual laws that work which will not be broken.) if you spend enough time in the Proverbs, you will see that a large percentage of all verses on the mouth will have the heart in them, and vice versa.

Lk. 6
"For out of the abundance of the heart, the mouth speaks."

Rms. 10
For with the heart man believes unto Righteousness,
And with the tongue confession is made unto Salvation.

Even so, the tongue is a little member and boasts great things. Behold how great a matter a little fire kindle. And the tongue is a fire, a world of iniquity: so is our tongue among our members; it defiles our whole body, and sets on fire the course of human nature and is set on the fire of hell.

Ps. 120
Deliver our soul, O Lord from lying lips, and from a deceitful tongue (in word and food).
What shall be given to you, or what shall be done to you, you false tongue?
Sharp arrows of the warrior, with coals of the broom tree.

Ps. 52
God will destroy you (the tongue) forever.
He will take you away, and pluck you out of your dwelling place, and uproot you from the land of the living.

There are few who understand the workings or the ramifications of the tongue, an entire world of its own.

Ps. 73
They set their mouth against the heavens, and their tongue walks (leads them) through the earth.

Remember, by your words, you will be justified, and by your words, you will be condemned.

Ps. 12
The Lord shall cut off all flattering lips and the tongue that speaks proud things.
Who lie (even to themselves) to their hearts content saying,
"With our tongue we will prevail, our lips are our own:
Who is Lord over us? Who can stop Us?
(Jesus, the Lord of angel armies, that who?)

Jn. 6:63
The Word of God (in my mouth) is Spirit and Life.

The Word of the Lord has come unto Us! Even the Word of God, which stands eternal in the heavens, which has been hiding for ages and generations, but is now made known to His saints ("Whomsoever will") that is, Christ in Us, the hope of glory! In the beginning was the Word, and the Word was with God, and the Word is God.

And the Word became flesh, and now lives in Us.
For He is dressed in a robe dipped in Blood,
and His name is called the Word of God.

The Word of Life in Us is alive, quick, and powerful!

Therefore, the Word of Life delivered by a tamed (Fasted) tongue and clean blood and belly is prophetic: Every time! Whether it feels like it or not.

The communication of Your faith firing up every good thing in You, in Christ, as a king–queen, reigning on Your throne of judgment (the will) over Your soul and body, scattering all evil with Your eyes (of the hidden Man of the heart), as a Stranger in the earth with holy flesh (blood and belly).

Ps. 103
He satisfies my mouth with good things and renews my youth like the eagle (always young in His presence).

Meditating the Word (Jesus) is a direct Spiritual feed to the Inner Man! For a man's belly (the spirit- the Christ in them) is satisfied by the fruit of his mouth, and by the increase of his lips (both outer and Inner), he is filled. For the power of life and death reside in the tongue. And since the Love of God is poured into Our hearts by the Holy Spirit, therefore, "out of the abundance of the heart, my mouth speaks."

The goal of the mouth is to get to a Place (Tamed – Fasted - tongue) where the answer of the Tongue is always from the Lord. That the tongue may speak of judgment (their Spiritual inherence), and the mouth brings forth Wisdom; for Jesus is Our wisdom. The Tamed tongue is the Tool of Our Trade and the Divine instrument for God's high praises.

Ps. 45:1
Our tongue as the pen of God!
Writing the Word of Life on the tablet of Our hearts. (Pro. 3:3)

Jer. 15
If you take away the vile (outer man) from the precious (Inner Man),
then, will you be as My mouth?

The Lord wants to pour out His grace upon Our lips. He wants to enrich Us in all knowledge and speech! For the divine Sentence is upon Our lips, as We teach (Fast) the mouth, through the Word and Fasting not to transgress!

You do not want the Children's voice of words to be hard, nor crooked, nor a lack of Words (of God)! The Proverbs will reveal God's standard of hard and crooked talk, which is much higher and deeper than the world's standard! Keep a tight leash on their tongue and tame the wild things, thus taming their life.

Why? The power of Life and death is in the tongue, and they that love (respect and tamed through Fasting), it will eat the fruit of it. (Good or bad)

Weaving the Words of Spirit and Life into a child's vocabulary should be paramount in the parent's life, for this is the Language of Heaven that will produce Milk and Honey (the Word) under their tongue, that they may know to choose the good, and to hate un-Godliness (evil).

Ps. 50
To Him who orders His conversation (life) aright, will l show the Salvation of God.

Feeding instead of reading the Bread of Life will mature the inner Man quickly, with a Spiritual understanding that will enlighten the eyes of their heart to see the glory of their inner Man – "Christ in Them, the hope of glory"!

Pro. 18
The belly (spirit) of a man shall be satisfied by the fruit of the mouth, and by the increase of the lips, they are filled. For the power of life and death is in the tongue, and they that love (respect- Fast) it, will eat the fruit of it (Good or bad).

The Bread of Life is Spirit and Life; it is designed to be Eaten, and when swallowed and digested through meditation (mental and verbal confession), produces the fruit of Spirit and Life, for the belly is satisfied by the fruit of the mouth, and by the increase of the lips the soul is filled.

The Bread of Life is designed to be eaten with the mouth (mental confession) of the Inward Man, not so much read. For the belly (spirit) is satisfied by the fruit of the mouth, not so much the eyes!

Rev. 10
I went up to the angel, and said to him, give Me the little Book. And he said to Me, take It and Eat it up. It will make Your belly bitter, but in Your mouth sweet as honey.

Jer. 15
Father, I found Your words and did Eat Them; They are unto Me a joy and rejoicing in My heart. (And a strength and a strengthening in My soul; and a filling and a fulfilling in My body.)

Job 23
Oh Jesus, I have esteemed the Words of Your mouth more than My necessary Food. Feed Me with food that is convenient for Me, lest I be full and deny You!

Mt. 4
Therefore, I do not live by the Word of God alone, but by bread also. (My translation)

Heb. 7
For the Word of the oath (Bible), which was since the law, makes the son, who is consecrated forever.

The mouth is God's divine utensil for Feeding the "hidden Man of the heart." For the Words in a man's mouth are as dainty morsels that go down into the innermost part of the being and, coupled together with the power of Life in the Tongue, provide a rich, deep Feed for the Inner Man that will outweigh the outer man in all things, which results in the Christ in You – Your hope of glory.

But I state My cause against you, and your grandchildren, that you have exchanged My glory for that which is of no value.

God's divine design for our mouth is to be like His mouth in creativity, power, and the high praises of God. Jesus did all His healing and miracles with Words (tamed-Fasted-tongue), His mouth being the only tool of His trade. The mouth of the righteous brings forth Wisdom and the tongue talks of judgment! This same Wisdom of God in Christ, in Me, that created the heavens, which is why we want to keep our mouth and our tongue always in check.

Pro. 12
The tongue of the Wise is healing.

A Child's mouth is their vehicle of Faith. Their mouth is God's divine utensil for Feeding their "hidden Man of the heart," writing the Word of Life on the tablet (paper) of their heart, and tuning their hearts to the Voice (Word) of the Lord.

The goal for their mouth is the Law of kindness on their tongues as a platform for the Wisdom of God. While their hearts are being stirred by a noble theme as they prophesy (confess) the Word of Life to their King.

For the Word of God is as deep waters, and the wellspring of Wisdom (of God) as a flowing brook, sweet to the soul, and health to all the bones. It would a tragedy for the Children to miss all this! You do not want their mouth set against the heavens, or themselves, or their neighbor.

Pro. 10
Wise men lay-up knowledge, but the mouth of fool is near destruction.

Oh Lord God of Heaven and earth, let all the Words of Our mouths and the feelings (meditation) of Our hearts be acceptable in Your sight!

May Our lip of Truth feed many and be established forever.

The Word will help to tame the tongue, and the taming of the tongue (inner Man) will result in the full control of the outer man, which will result in peace and joy - total victory.

Song of Solomon 4
A Garden enclosed is my sister my spouse.
A spring shut up and a fountain sealed:
A fountain of gardens, and a well of Living waters.

The Devil's arena is the flesh (with its feelings and desires), and he wants to shut up the outer man in his arena, the carnal flesh. If you shut down the flesh (Fasting – tongue), you shut down the Battle!

A Tamed tongue = A Tamed Life (spirit, soul, and body).

A Good man is satisfied by Himself - building Himself up on His most holy faith by praying in the Spirit with a holy, tamed tongue. The Spirit Himself is building up the inner Man into the Image of Christ, with groanings that cannot be uttered!

Fasting is the quickest and easiest way to take the vile (un-Godliness) away from the precious (Christ in You). The other option is a long, drawn-out fight of trials and errors, taking a lifetime to sort out. Just 5 small years of Fasting did more for me in the taking away (and understanding) of the vile than 30 years of Christianity without Fasting. Fasting deals with the Interior (tongue and Living waters), renovating the belly and blood for the Living waters of God, and taming the tongue so that it may bear the full weight of the Wisdom of God.

The mouth is very complicated, containing the power of death to destroy your life or the power of Life to deliver the Wisdom of God. The outer man is a veil enclosing the inner Man. The outer man, in his fallen state, has no interest in God (which is vile) and is continually trying to suppress the inner Man, the Image of God – the Precious –the Christ in You - Your hope of glory.

Fasting will totally shut down the outer man – reviving the "hidden Man of the heart" to subdue and lead (with gladness and joy) the outer man into the fat pastures (Eternal life) of God.

Ecc 2.

He that labors works for himself; for his mouth craves it of him.

P.S

Ecc. 5

Guard your steps when you go into the House of God, and be more ready to hear, than to give the sacrifice of fools: for they consider not that they do evil.

Be not rash with your mouth, and let not your heart be hasty to utter anything before God:

For God is in Heaven, and you are upon the earth: therefore, let your words be few. For in the multitude of dreams and many words, are many vanities: but you fear God!

<u>*Mouth – Meditation #1*</u>

Theme

Jn. 6:63

THE WORD OF GOD IN MY MOUTH IS SPIRIT AND LIFE

Pro. 18:20-21

My belly shall be satisfied by the fruit (Words) of My mouth
and by the increase of My lips shall I be filled.

For the power of life and death is in My tongue,
and I will eat the fruit of it.

Jer. 15:1

Therefore, if I take away the vile from the Precious,
then, shall My mouth be as the mouth of God.

Introduction

Ps. 12:1-4

Help, O Lord, for the Godly are fast disappearing,
and the faithful have vanished from the earth.
Empty and false are man's words to his fellow. they talk with flattering lips
and a double mind. The Lord shall cut off all flattering lips
and the tongue that speaks proud things.
Who lie to their hearts content,
saying,
"With our tongue we will prevail,
our lips are our own:
Who is Lord over us? Who can stop us?

Ps. 73:9

They set their mouth against the heavens, and their tongue walks through the earth.

Hosea 7:16
They shall fall by the Sword because of the rage of their tongues.

Content

1.

Jn. 6

THE WORD OF GOD IN MY MOUTH IS SPIRIT AND LIFE.

Ps. 45

For My tongue is the pen of God!

Pro. 3

Engraving the Word of God on the tablet (paper) of My heart.

Pro. 31

Therefore, My tongue will speak with the law of kindness.

2.

Pro.8

All the words of My mouth are in righteousness,
and there is nothing crooked or hard in them.

Pro.10

My tongue is as choice silver, for Jesus is My righteousness.

Ps. 45

Therefore, grace is poured out on My lips.

Pro. 10

My mouth is a well of Life.

3.

Ps. 17

I AM:
purposed so that My mouth will not transgress!

Pro. 18

All the words in My mouth are as deep waters
and the wellspring of Wisdom as a flowing brook.

S.O,S.

My lips also drop as the Honeycomb,
Milk and Honey are under My tongue.

Pro. 15

Therefore, My wholesome (Tamed) tongue is a tree of Life.

4

Pro. 10

My mouth brings forth Wisdom; for Jesus is My Wisdom.

Pro. 12

Idle talk can pierce like a sword, but the tongue of the Wise is healing.

Pro.16:

Pleasant anointed words are as a honeycomb,
sweet to the soul, and health to all the bones.

Pro. 12:

I AM:
Filled with good as a result of My words.

5.

1 Sam.

My mouth is pulled over My enemies, because I rejoice in Your salvation.

Ps. 39

I will watch how I behave, so that I will not sin with My mouth.

I will put a muzzle (Fasting) on My mouth
whenever I am confronted with evil.

Ps. 141:3

I will set a watch over My mouth, Jesus, and keep the door of My lips!

1 Pt. 3:3-4

Let not the adorning be that of the outward man, the braiding of hair,
and the wearing of gold or the putting on of apparel:

But let it be the "hidden Man of the heart", in that which is not corruptible, even the
ornament of a meek and quiet spirit, which is in the sight of God is of great price.

Summary

Rm. 5:5

The love of God is poured into My heart by the Holy Spirit, which is given to Me,

Lk. 6 :45

For out of the abundance of My heart My mouth speaks.

Pro. 16:1

Therefore, the answer of My tongue is always from the Lord.

P.S.

Ps. 51:15

Open My lips, Jesus, and My mouth will show forth all Your praise.

Pro. 12:19

My lip of Truth will feed many and be established forever!

Ps. 19:17

Let the words of My mouth and the meditation of My heart
be acceptable in Your sight, O Lord!

The Mouth – Meditation #2

Theme

Ps. 57:4, 6

My soul is among lions: I lie even among them that are set on fire,
even the sons of men, whose teeth are spears and arrows,
and their tongue a sharp sword.

Mt. 12:37

By My words I will be justified, and by My words I will be condemned.
(It is as simple as that!)

Introduction

Ps. 50:23

To Him who orders His conversation (life) aright,
will l show the Salvation of God.

Ps.71:23-24

My lips shall greatly rejoice when I sing unto You;
and My soul which You have redeemed.
My tongue also shall speak of Your righteousness
all day long.

1 Cor. 1:5

I AM: enriched in all knowledge and speech!

Content

1

Pro. 6:12

A naughty person, a wicked man, walks with crooked (froward) speech.

Pro. 20:17

Bread of deceit is sweet to a man, but afterwards
his mouth will be filled with gravel.

Pro. 14:3

But the lips of the wise will protect them.

Pro. 15:1

A gentle answer always turns away wrath because Love never fails!

Pro. 25:15

With patience a ruler may be won over,
and a gentle tongue can break the bone.

Pro. 10:10

Where there be many words, sin is present,
but he who refrains his lips is Wise.

Pro. 15:28

My mind of righteousness always thinks before speaking.

Pro. 11:12

A man of understanding holds his peace.

3

Pro. 17:28

Even a fool, when he holds his peace, is counted Wise,
and he that shuts his lips, is esteemed a man of understanding.

Jm. 1:19

I AM: swift to hear - slow to speak – and slow to wrath!

Pro. 19:9

A false witness will not go unpunished, and he that speaks lies will perish.

Pro. 29:20
See a man hasty in his words?
There is more hope for a fool than for him.

4

Ps. 119

I hate and abhor lying, but Your law do I love.

Ps. 12:3

The Lord will cut off the flattering lips and the proud tongue.

Ps. 119:43

Take not Your word of Truth utterly out of My mouth, Jesus.
(May I always retain the Wisdom of God.)

Ps. 119

Remove from Me a lying tongue and grant Me Your law graciously.

Heb.13:15
I will offer My sacrifices of praise to God continually, that is,
the fruit of My lips giving thanks to His name.

Summary

Pro. 16:10

The Divine sentence is on My lips, therefore,
My mouth shall not transgress in judgment.

1 Cor. 1:5

I AM: enriched in all knowledge and speech!

P.S.

Ps. 109:18

As he loved cursing so let it come to him:
as he delighted not in blessing, let it be far from him.

Pro. 18:18

The words in a man's mouth are as dainty morsels
that go down into the innermost part of his being.

Chapter 12

Spiritual Warfare

Rev. 12: 7-9
*There was war in Heaven: Michael and his angels fought against the Dragon.
And the Dragon fought the angels and lost, and had no more place in Heaven
and the great Dragon was cast out, that old serpent, called the Devil and Satan,
which deceives the whole world: he was cast out into earth with his angels.*

Rev. 12: 12
*…woe to you that inhabit the earth and the sea, for the Devil is come down
unto you, having great wrath because he knows he has but a short time.*

Eph. 6: 10-17
*Therefore, my brethren, be strong in the Lord, and in the power of his might. Put on
the whole armour of God, that ye may be able to stand against the wiles of the devil.*

*For we wrestle not against flesh and blood, but against principalities,
against powers, against the rulers of the darkness of this world,
against spiritual wickedness in high places.*

*Wherefore take unto you the whole armour of God,
that ye may be able to withstand in the evil day,
and having done all, to stand.*

*Stand therefore, having your loins girt about with Truth, and having
on the breastplate of righteousness, and your feet shod with
the preparation of the gospel of peace.*

*Above all, taking the shield of Faith, wherewith ye shall be able to
quench all the fiery darts of the wicked.*

*And take the helmet of Salvation, and the Sword of the Spirit, which is the Word of God:
praying always, with all prayer and supplication in the Spirit, and watching
with all perseverance and supplication for all saints.*

Jer. 17:12
A glorious high throne from the beginning is the place of Our sanctuary.

Heb. 4:16
Let Us therefore come boldly to the Throne of Grace!

There is definitely a Spiritual war going on right now, at this very moment, in every Christian's life!

And the Father has chosen this "Good fight of Faith" to be fought in an unseen arena of Faith. We do not physically see this spiritual enemy, for it would be overwhelming and unfair for the common Christian, and it would not increase Our faith: Israel seen many miracles and it did not increase their Faith.

Thus, an invisible Battle for the "perfecting of the Saints", as the "evidence of things not seen". And this Battle will go on in our souls until the day we die, for the perfection of our souls will continue until then. God is planning an eternal excellence for Zion, the Body of Christ (You) !

Ps. 119: 98
You have made me wiser than my enemies,
which are forever with me (in all aspects of the Christian life).

The Father allows a daily Battle in order to train His Children 's (Judges 3: 2) hands for war (for Love) and their fingers to fight (for Love and Faith). God told Joshua and David to leave a portion of the enemy (giants) that Children of Israel might know war. The Lord of Hosts has two swords for the sharpening of the Saints: the Word of God, and the wicked (Ps. 17:3): which keep Us sharp. It is a good fight because Jesus (Our big Brother) has already spoiled all principalities and powers that be, and provided Us with all the Judgments of the Word of His power declared against the wicked in the Psalms. Remember, Jesus is the Head, and We (the Church) are His body, and joint-Heirs with Christ, in all things.

This is a "good fight of Faith" because Jesus has already provided the victory for Us in the Spirit, before the foundations of the world: but We (the Church) need to translate this victory of Jesus into this world, by the Word (Judgments against the wicked) of His power and the Spirit of holiness.

Ps. 9:5
You have rebuked the heathen: You have destroyed the wicked,
You have put out their name forever.

It's our game, bat and ball, and Jesus (the Word) is the Umpire, therefore, no worries!

However, this daily Spiritual battle is very foreign to the meek, forgiving, spirit of a Christian pilgrim. So, the idea of warfare is usually ignored and shuffled off to the side, along with Fasting! Instead of fighting the good fight of Faith. Therefore, most Christians have no spiritual warfare in their lives, which is a sure sign of a "shipwrecked Faith". For the Lord is daily pruning His branches (Children) to Perfection. Most Christians see themselves as Citizens of Heaven, always loving their neighbors and their enemies, not soldiers, thus a dilemma in their soul.

Ps.13
Oh Lord, how long shall I cherish this daily grief in My soul?

It's not easy to reconcile the Fruits of the Spirit in the character of a Christian with the mental attitude of warring in the arena of Spiritual warfare, with the unseen, which is the other end of the spectrum. The Fruits of the Spirit do not come cheaply. We need to daily fight this jealous enemy to preserve our Fruits in Christ Jesus. This is the forging of the Saints into pure gold.

How did David reconcile in His soul: all the aggressive bloodshed fought during the day with all the ungodly nations around him (the will of God), and then in the evening, fellowship with the Father and writing sweet Psalms of the Lord?

By Faith, that's how!

Just like Us today, by laying aside Our dirty robes of righteousness by (Faith in God), and putting on the Garment of Praise (strength), to still the enemy and the Avenger. Spiritual warfare always bring Us back to the Blood, For We cannot even start without washing in the Blood of Jesus: too much condemnation.

Yes, the Sweet Psalmist of Israel is a Man Of War.
The gracious Lord Himself is a Man of War.
The Church (His Body) needs to be a People of war!

Our New Creation (Christ in You, Your hope of glory) of God is to be fashioned and moulded by Love and Spiritual warfare (faith). Christians need to learn how to switch gears from Lovers to Fighters (for the sake of Love and the world) by Faith in the Blood of Jesus and the Word of His power. Once cleansed by the Blood of the Lamb You are instantaneously "as He is in this world", and qualified to declare all the Judgments of the Lord against the wicked.

You will experience a great amount of peace as the enemy flees all the Judgments of the Lord coming out of Your mouth against them! For all the Judgments of the Lord are God's words, not Yours: quickening all kinds of Faith in Your soul.

Most Christians today are not fighting but just barely hanging on to Their salvation (due to a lack of Fasting), never mind warring against an unseen enemy: meanwhile the Father has provided Us with ample ammunition, and peace: even the Word of His power, the Sword of the Lord, which is able to slice through anything in its path. And with it, We are more than conquerors, through Him that loved Us, and washed Us in His own blood. The Body of Christ needs to be taking more ground, moving forward to destroy the works of the Devil, on behalf of Our neighbours and the world: as Shields of the earth and Ambassadors of Heaven. This is why Jesus came to the earth!

1 Jn. 3
For this purpose, was the Son of God (Body of Christ) manifested, that He should destroy the works of the devil.

And Fasting (clean blood), with the Sword of the Lord (the Word) in Your hand will definitely do the Job. All these Judgments against the wicked in the Psalms reveal the reality of their downfall, and the reality Our uprising, which quickens the Faith of God in Us, not only to squash the enemies in Our lives, but to also move every mountain in Our lives, and the lives of others who are hurting: thus destroying the works of the Devil!

My Testimony

Ps. 144
Blessed be the Lord that trains My hands for war (Love) and My fingers to fight (Faith).

I was a daily practising Christian for over 20 years before I grasped the "warfare" of the Scriptures. I was also a struggling Christian, with not much holiness because of no Fasting.

Then in 2010 the Lord led me into Psalms 119 for a season. (I just could not stop to this day, years later – it is My daily staple).

This Psalm with all its many "I wills" strengthened My will power to be able to say yes, when the Father called me to Fasting.

(63 Fasts ago - see my Fasting book "Fearfully and Wonderfully made").

Then, through Fasting , the Lord led me into the Psalms, revealing to me the 4 different categories of the Psalms -

WORSHIP (Character and Providence)

THE "CRY" (Prayer)

OUR INHERITANCE. (Identification and Eternal Life)

WARFARE.

This is how the Captain of my Faith began training my hands for war and my fingers to fight for the Spiritual warfare of the Psalms (the Judgments of the Lord) against the wicked, which by the way, has passed through all three heavens.

Satan and his bunch are already sentenced and judged!

We just need to get onboard God's will.

Ps. 9:5
You have rebuked the heathen: You have destroyed the wicked, You have put out their name forever.

Ps. 119: 119
You put away all the wicked like dross (garbage), and that's why I love (obey) your law.

This warfare of the Psalms upgraded my Character and prayer life to a whole new level, ushering in the Reality of the duty of My office as a "Shield of the earth" and enriching Me with identification and purpose: always looking to execute the judgments of My new-found office.

Ps. 47:9
The princes of the peoples, are gathered-together, even the People (Church - Body of Christ) of the God of Abraham, for the Shields of the earth belong to God.

But what if I would have said no to Ps. 119 or Fasting, and stopped along the Way? I had to take courage many a time, especially for the Fasting! The first season of My Spiritual warfare took a toll on My soul: it was hard to wrap my head around God's judgments: and always having to Wash on a daily basis was overwhelming! I had to use Tongues often because of lingering condemnation after Washing.

Washing in the Blood of Jesus on a daily basis caused me to grow in Faith in the blood for total righteousness which is required for the declarations of God judgments. You do not have to be perfect to declare the Judgments of the Lord, just clean (Righteous), in the Blood of Jesus.

There is no expiration date on the Blood of Jesus, and We can use it as much, and as long as We want to combat this daily Spiritual warfare. The enemy attacks for no cause at all, all day long, therefore, if needs be, we can wash in the blood of Jesus, all day long, if We have to.

To get right back into declaring the "Judgments of the Lord" (which are sweeter than honey and better than money) as the Righteousness of God: as He is in this world.

For the Devil will immediately get busy at tearing You down as a Shield of the earth. The Blood always gives Us the victory in Christ Jesus! It is designed that way. Use the blood as often as you want, as often as it takes to regain your Faith (Righteousness): as often as the enemy attacks.

Spiritual warfare also requires a Blow for blow, and Word for word combat in all confrontations of unbelief (just like Jesus did in the desert with the Devil): with your immediate response of the Word of His power!

This same attitude is to be used with your Tongue (which is the hand that holds the Sword) and your daily words. The judgments of the Lord need to be delivered off a tamed (Fasting) tongue, for the power of life and death is in the Tongue. The success of Your warfare hinges on Your consistent ability to deliver Blow for blow and Word for Word combat to the Devil.

Do not let anything go by, both in Word and deed, wash it all out.

Christians need to learn how to switch gears from Lovers to fighters by the Faith in the Blood of Jesus and personal experience in Spiritual warfare with the Word of His power. Theses Judgments shed a lot of Light on the enemy which helped Me avoid all the paths of the Destroyer, and to walk freely in the in the Light, as He is in the Light!

Pro. 22
A Wise (a Believer) man sees evil coming and hides Himself (in Christ - the Word), but the foolish pass on and are punishment.

Pro. 20
A Wise man sifts out the wicked and brings the Wheel (Word) over them.

The spiritual warfare of Psalms reveal the character and tactics of the enemy, You can get to know Your enemy!

More time in warfare = Understanding = the Reality of the enemies downfall, and Our uprising!

Experience in the Psalms warfare (up ahead) generates Kingdom Faith through the blend of Your Spiritual kingly Identification, and Satan's pronounced judgments: their documented downfall.

In Spiritual warfare, We need to go (by Faith) from a nobody, begging mode, to a Shield of the earth squashing mode, via the declarations of all the judgments of the Lord against the ungodly.

To be able to move from a Lover to a fighter: from an Ambassador of Heaven to a " Shield of the earth", at the first sign of trouble!

Ps. 119: 20
My soul breaks, for the longing that it has, for Your judgments at all times!

It takes a skilled swordsman to wield the Sword of the Lord (the Word of His power): it is heavy and very sharp, especially when praying the raw Word of His power for hours.

Jer. 48
Cursed be the Man that keeps His sword (the Word) from blood (from fighting the "good fight of Faith).

Ps. 48
Let mount Zion rejoice and let the Daughters of Judah be glad, because of Your judgments.

Isa. 59
As for Me, this is My covenant with Them, says the Lord,
My Spirit which is upon You, and My words which I have put in Your mouth,
will not depart out of Your mouth, nor out of the mouth of Your seed,
nor out of the mouth of Your seed 'seed,
says the Lord, from now on, and forevermore.

Duet. 6
These Words that I command You this day will be in Your heart.
You will teach them diligently to Your children, and
will talk of them when You sit in Your house,
and when You walk in the way,
when You lie down, and
when You rise-up.

Ps. 132
"If Your children will keep My covenant and My testimony that I will teach Them,
then Their children will also sit upon Your throne!

Who champion My will cause against the wicked?
Who will stand up for Me against the evil doers?

I will.

PRAYER - Meditation # 1

Theme

Ps. 47:9

The Prince's (believing Christians) of the peoples have gathered Themselves together
as the People of the God of Abraham (Body of Christ);
for the Shields of the earth belong to God.

Introduction

Rev. 8:3-5

Another angel came and stood at the altar, having a golden censer;
and there was given unto him much incense,
that he should offer it up with the Prayers of all the Saints
upon the golden alter which was before the Throne.

And the smoke of the incense, which came
with the Prayers of all the Saints,
ascended up before God out of the angel's hand.

The angel took the censer, and filled it with the fire of the altar
and cast it unto the earth:

And there were voices, thundering, lightning and an earthquake.

Jm. 5:16

THE PRAYER'S OF A RIGHTEOUS MAN AVAILS MUCH!

Content

Jn. 16:23

In that day You shall ask Me nothing.
Truly, truly, I say unto You, whatsoever You
shall ask the Father in My name, He will give it to You.

Job 22

I will also decree a thing, and it shall be established unto Me,
and the Light will shine on My ways.

Heb. 4:10

I will come boldly unto the Throne of Grace!

Isa. 41:1

Keep silence before Me, O Islands; and let the People renew their
strength: let Them come near; then let Them speak:
let Us come near to Judgment.

Rm. 8:26

Likewise, the Spirit (of God) also helps Me with My weaknesses.

Isa. 43:26

Put Me (God) in remembrance: let Us plead together, says the Lord:
You declare; that You may be justified.

Mt. 18:18

Whatsoever I bind on earth shall be bound in heaven:
and whatsoever I loose on earth shall be loosed in heaven.

Isa. 45:11

Thus, says the Lord, the Holy One of Israel, and His Maker,
ask of Me about the things to come.

1 Cor. 12:12

Our help is in the Name (Jesus) of the Lord, which made Heaven and earth.

I AM: A co-laborer together with God!

Pro. 12:19

My Lip of Truth shall be established forever!

Summary

Isa. 62:6

I AM: a Watchman on Your walls, O Jerusalem,
I will: never hold My peace day or night:
I will: make mention of the Lord;
I will: not keep not silent.
I will: give Him no rest,
till He establish,

and till He make Jerusalem a praise in the earth.

Go through, go through the gates; prepare ye the Way of the people;
cast up, cast up the Highway (holiness).

Isa. 62:1

For Zion's sake I will not hold my peace and for Jerusalem's sake
I will not rest
until the Righteousness thereof goes for as the brightness,
and the Salvation thereof as a lamp that burns.

P.S.

Pro. 28:4

He that forsakes the Law (of holiness) gives praise to the wicked!

159

The Fruits of Fasting

It is hard for Me to convey the following testimony without sounding like an arrogant fool: but I guess We are all "fools for Christ sake", one time or another, to the glory of God the Father!

How to feed My inner man.

After 7 days of Fasting doing My daily devotionals the rest of the Bible goes down easy on a fully loaded body, including labours of Love. This also taught me how to meditate producing enough spiritual stamina to juggle 15-20 precious Promises at a time (a meditation) from My book "Blueprints for Meditation".

The Lord sometimes blending different meditations together: forging a cross reference of the Word in my mind of Christ (mental capacity). No boredom anymore, I rejoice in the dance (meditation) as a Child (holy) of God! Also feeding on the "Zion series" from the same book with its 10 meditations on the Church which is the Body of Christ, which is the City of God.

Keeping the Word of His power

One of the cries of Ps. 119 is "I will keep Your word". After 8 years of declaring this phrase I find Myself keeping the Word of God for me, and my family. I also find myself keeping everything and anything! The Word of God is incorruptible Seed - just plant it in your heart and it will grow!

Keeping God's alphabet of Life (Psalm119) works very well for the children and teenagers as well. The short, potent, 8 verses of the Will of God for that day are sustaining for the kids and yourself when at your lowest point of Faith!

If you can keep the simple 8 verses of Ps. 119 daily for 22 days (a small season), then, you will be well on your way in keeping your Salvation until you get to Heaven. For Ps. 119 is a springboard to keeping the entire Word of His power. Psalm 119 is a daily execution of the Will of God for the day, and 22 day season. Keeping this Psalm daily gave me the power, desire and confidence (Faith) to be as He is in this world, even as beloved Child of the Most High.

My daughter Jaylah

Me and Jaylah (12 years old) have been in this Feed below daily for 8 years weaving the Word of His power into Her vocabulary as the Lord continues to light Her candle (spirit) with Spiritual understanding. Soon after I committed Myself to the Psalm, the Lord had Me feed it to my daughters, daily, and faithfully the last 8 years!

As of November 2021

Me and Jayah have been in the Word for approximately 8 years now.

She has been through the full:

Psalms 119   -   96 times (1 prayer a day)

Psalms   -   16 times (1 a day)

Proverbs   -   96 times (1 a day)

Gospels   -   96 times (1 chapter a day) (rotating all 4 Gospels)

The Letters   -   (3 year now - 1 chapter a day)

All in about 1 hour a day.

Pro. 8
A wise man discerns both time and judgment.

I have done much discerning with both time and judgment over the years, by making the right decisions (executing judgment) for the Word of Life, to keep their Spiritual feed through the day, every day! Hardest thing I ever did, but worth it all: for that forever Stuff. It pays off to park in God's word!

Mental and Spiritual capacity for My eternal time-line (Word schedule)!

Gospels

(1 per week)

1 chapters a day for 3 years now; Mathew the 1st week - Mark the 2nd week - etc. Daily and faithfully, (for the most part of the Course) – there are however, "those days". My soul breaking for the longing that it has for His judgments at all times.

(First thing in the morning with the Master!)

Proverbs

Proverbs 1 on the 1st day of the month

Proverbs 2 on the 2nd, etc. (faithfully for years now, since the Psalm)

And faithfully rotating (every other month) to the Scriptures of proverbs on the mouth, the fool, and the Wise, (that I charted out): the Wise the 1st week - the fool the 2nd week - the mouth the 3rd week – the Fear of the Lord 4th week.

Psalms

In the same fashion – Psalms 1 on the 1st - Psalms 2 on the 2nd (faithfully for years now – since this Psalm. With all the Scriptures that pronounce the judgments of God against the wicked, (that I charted out): Prophesying them frequently on behalf of My family and Church, co-laboring together in the work of the Lord, by the Spirit of the Word.

Old Testament

1 chapter a day systematically, in one forward direction, (since this Psalm).

Epistles

1 chapter a day systematically, in one forward direction, since this Psalm.

Prophets

Which is no easy park: one at a time, months at a time, with coinciding meditations.

The Zion series: 1 – 10

("Blueprints for Meditation")

Praying and meditating them a couple days before church. 1 per week (with a month break after week 8) - 3 times a year.

Nurturing a serious, mature Burden of the Word and an understanding of Zion, which is the Church, which is the Body of Christ, a world without end.

This Psalm will give you all the Spiritual stamina You need: as far as your Eye (spirit) can see. Giving Me a full scope of the Word of God in My life; for the Word is My fortress, where unto I may continually resort.

All in about 2 hours (Spread throughout the day if working). Not including Daughter's discipleship: 1-2 hours mixed with all activities – "redeeming the time as a Wise man discerning (understanding) both time and judgment."

Written 4 books

(Thanks to Fating!)

This Psalm has produced the Spiritual stamina and inspiration to write 4 books!

Never written anything before this Psalm.

"God's Divine Alphabet"
(A Whole Heart)

"Gods' Peculiar Treasurers"
(Parents manual for the Children's spiritual feed)

"Fearfully and Wonderfully made" - the Fasting Book
(From five-year Fasting diary).

"Blueprints for Meditation"
Over 100 meditations with the Scriptures falling in their Divine sequence; some taking years to fall. They are the Divine curriculum for My Christian school The Joshua Generation – 50% Spiritual and 50% scholastic.

Never did much of anything until Psalms 119 and Fasting - (thanks to 119).

All this from poor little old Me: Bored and wandering around aimlessly in the Word. Psalm 119 has weaved the Will (Word) of God into My natural life and vocabulary (Me and the Word are one)! We need to go from a half hour Feed (confessing- meditation), to one hour Feed - to two hour Feed, and so on. To make Our souls fat, and flourishing for the earth, Our neighbour, and the Kingdom of God.

Fasting

44 Fasts in 10 years - 1 fast every 3 months, with many missed meals (sacrifices) between Fasts; and also maintaining pure blood by eating from true hunger to true hunger (2nd or 3rd hunger pain). The last 3 Fasts being major fasts, over 21 days (not to mention the many physical blessings, including the holy flesh). "For the paths of the Lord drop with fatness" (Ps.) "And the Dew lay all night on my branches" (Job).

(See my book "Fearfully and Wonderfully made")

Will power for daily faithfulness

I have awakened in the morning (after following Jesus up a high mountain) declaring, "I'm not doing anything today"; but I soon find Myself running in the path His commandments again, because of the holy momentum of this Psalm that is in Me.. I get up early if working, to keep His word; 1 bring a meditation with Me to work to pray. I never leave home without a med!

Flipped My soul and body

From the bitter to the Sweet. I'm talking about being "stirred by a noble Theme", about delighting, rejoicing, respecting - keeping unto the End - running the full Course in the high Calling of God, as a Steward (keeper) of the Mysteries of God! This Psalm will straighten you out and sharpen You up!

Upgraded My down time

From going 2 hrs. to 4 hrs. in the Will of God, to all day, and sometimes even into the night, not being able to fall asleep because of the Quickening,and the roasting of the meditations, "being stuck to His testimonies". Sometimes I have to ask the Father to turn it off, so I can sleep. "Have you found some Honey (Word)? don't eat too much, lest you be full and vomit.

Ears to Hear

This Psalm of Psalms gave me an ear to hear the Voice of the Lord which now thunders upon My waters (soul). He awakens Me morning by morning to hear as the Learned. All that faith coming by hearing, and surely accumulating unto the full measure of the stature of Christ. (Wow!)

Patience

This Psalm provided a Good place to park in the Word for its season - without being side tracked – keeping the Word. This is My 10th year, daily, in this one Psalm. How's that for waiting on the Lord (Word).

The Word speaking

When I sleep, the Word keeps Me! When I awaken the Word speaks to Me, and when I go the Word leads Me.

Understanding

I can smell the understanding of whatever book of the Bible I'm in.

Iron will (Sceptre)

From Fasting inspired by the keeping of this Psalm (Word - will of God).

Tamed tongue

From many confessions (personal pronouns) and the humbling of Fasting: because of the Psalm.

Rotating

The Word, the Will of God, and labors of Love.

Sometimes the Word taking a back seat to labours of love, and vice versa.

Intercession

From periodically - to a regular half hour - to 1 hour - to hours - to a state of being!

Holy flesh

Delivered from 3 idols (including a sin consciousness) in My life, looking and expecting the power of God because of the understanding of the holy flesh (Circumcision of Christ made without hands) that is in Psalm 119; both the getting of the holy flesh, and the keeping of it. The holy Word needs holy flesh to dwell in, or else, everything doesn't Fit – and the Word cannot become flesh!

Worship and intimacy

Meeting Him early in the Garden (prayer), then off to soar the high places (worship) of the earth, and to feed on the Heritage of Jacob (the Word) upon the high mountains (meditations) of Israel, where I sit under His shadow with great delight. I had to climb the "hill of frankincense" (prayer), and the "mountain of myrrh" (Fasting) to get there!

Ecc.10
But the labour of the foolish wearies every one of them,
because they do not know how to get to the City of the great King.

Deep burden of the Lord

Now with a mature understanding of Zion (the Body of Christ), the fullness of all that fills all in all

(Thanks to the help of the Zion series from "Blueprints for Meditation".)

Expanded Horizon

I can see way past My nose now. The word "forever" has become a Reality to Me (a flashing neon sign)! Loving My enemies, doing good to them that despitefully use Me, praying for those who persecute Me, and suffering for His namesake! A COMMITTED 40 MINUTES and a season in this Psalm is an amazing springboard into the Wisdom of God! It will soar you up into the "high places."

Ps.119
Remember Your Word unto Your servant, upon which You have caused me to hope.

GOOD SEED INDEED!

Pro. 14
I AM: filled with good by the fruit of my mouth.

The incorruptible Seed of God! Just plant it; it will grow, you will grow!

High cleansing efficiency - daily body flush

After about 30 Fasts, or a low 20 % tox-level I find My body constantly, daily, flushing itself out lots of urine - throat flehm - and nose snot. A contestant excretion of undesirables from a high efficiency of a clean interior and blood.

Judgment Calls - Meditation #1

Theme

Ps. 94:16

Who will champion My cause against the wicked?
Who will stand up for Me against the evildoers?

I will.

Introduction

Jn. 3:8

For this purpose was the Son of God manifested, that He should destroy the works of the devil.

Ps. 80:1

Even the Son of Man (Me – "whomsoever will") which you have made strong for Yourself.

1 Jn. 2:6

If any Man says He abides in Christ, He should also walk even as He walked.

Content

P s. 58

Do You indeed speak Righteousness, oh congregation?
Do You judge uprightly, oh You sons of men.

In heart You work wickedness, yes,
you weigh the violence of your hands in the earth!

Jer. 5:

Run ye back and forth through the streets of Jerusalem,
and see now, and know, and seek in the broad places thereof.

If You can find a Man, if there be any that executes judgment,
that seeks the Truth; and I will pardon it!

Jer. 5: 4-

Surely These are poor, they are foolish, for They
know not the Way of the Lord, nor the
judgment of Their God.

Micah 3:1

Hear, I pray, oh You heads (Pastors) of Jacob (the Church), and
you princes (Christians) of the house of Israel (the Church).
Is it not for you to know judgment?

Pro. 29:4

For a king-queen (in Christ) by judgment establishes the land (Fruits of the Spirit),
but he who receives bribes overthrows it.

1 Cor. 6:2-3

Do You not know that the saints shall judge the world?
And if the world shall be judged by You,
are You unworthy to judge the smallest matters?

Do You not know that You shall judge angels?
How much more the things that pertain to this life?

(These Scriptures are written to the simple humble Christians in the Corinthian Church.)

Isa. 28

The Lord will be a Spirit of judgment for them that sit in judgment
and a source of strength for Them that turn the
battle to the gate (thanksgiving and praise).

Ps. 37

For My mouth brings forth Wisdom, and My tongue speaks of judgment!

Pro. 20:8

Therefore, I, as king - queen (over My soul and body),
sit on My throne (will) of judgment,
to scatter all evil with My eyes.

Ps. 9:5

You have rebuked the heathen, You have destroyed the wicked,
You have put out their name forever.

Ps. 7:6

Arise, Jesus, in Your anger, and lift-up Yourself because of the rage of
My enemies: awake for Me to the judgment You have commanded.

Pro. 11:1

A false balance is an abomination to the Lord: but a just weight is His delight.

Ps.119:108

Accept, We pray, the free will offerings of Our mouth,
and teach Us Your judgments!

Ps. 119:20

My soul cries out for the longing that it has for Your judgments at all times.

Ps. 119:6

At midnight,
I will rise to give thanks to You for Your righteous judgments (Our inheritance).

Summary

Pro. 14

For the evil must bow before the good, and the wicked at the gates of the Righteous.

Ps.. 149:6-9

*The high praise of God is in now My mouth, and a two-edged Sword
in My hand. To execute vengeance upon the heathen
and punishment upon the people.*

*To bind their kings (Rulers and principalities in heavenly places) with chains, their nobles
with fetters of iron. To execute upon them the judgment written:
This honor has all His saints.*

Ecc. 8:5

A Wise man's heart (My heart) discerns both time and judgment!

SUPPORT YOUR FAMILY – YOUR LOCAL CHURCH -

YOUR HOUSEHOLD OF FAITH (prayer list)

EVEN THE WHOLE BODY OF CHRIST IN PRAYER UNTO OUR GOD.

Psalms - Warfare

(120 minutes to pray)

1 Jn. 3:8
For this purpose was the Son of God (Me) manifested that He should destroy the works of the Devil.

Ps.119:98
You through Your commandments have made Me wiser than My enemies:
for they are forever with Me.

Book 1

(40 minutes)

Part a

Ps. 1
We are blessed because We do not walk in the counsel of the un-Godly,
nor stand in the way of sinners, nor sit in the seat of the scornful.
But Our delight is in the Law of the Lord, in which We
do meditate day and night.

We are like a tree planted by the rivers of water that brings forth fruit in Our season, and Our leaf will
not wither, and whatsoever We do will prosper.

But the un-Godly are not so, but are like the chaff that the wind drives away. Therefore, the un-Godly
will not stand in judgment (Godly righteousness – everlasting life), nor sinners in the Congregation of the
Righteous.

The Lord knows the way of the Righteous: but the way of the un-Godly will perish.

2: 4-5, 10-12
Why do the heathen rage and the people imagine a vain thing? The kings of the earth set themselves, and
the rulers take counsel together against the Lord and His anointed (Jesus and His body – the Church –
Zion – Me and You), saying,

"Let us break Their (the Church) bands in half and cast away Their cords from us" (not vice a versa).

He that sits in the heavens (all 3 heavens) will laugh: the Lord will have them in derision. Then will He
speak to them in His wrath, and vex them in their sore displeasure. Yet have I set My king (David – Jesus
- and Me in Him) upon My holy hill of Zion. I will declare the decree: The Lord has said unto me,

"You are My son (Jesus and His body the Church), this day have I begotten you.
Ask of Me,
and I will give You the heathen for your inheritance and the utter most parts of
the earth for your possession. You will break them with a rod of iron:
You will dash them into pieces like a potter's vessel."

2: 10-12

Be wise now, oh you kings: Be instructed you judges of the earth.
Serve the Lord with fear and rejoice with trembling. Kiss the Son,
lest He be angry, and you perish from the Way,
when His wrath is kindled but a little.

Blessed are all They that put their trust in Him.

Part b

3: 1-2
Lord how are they increased that trouble Us!
Many are they that rise-up against Us.
Many there be which say of Our soul,
"There is no help for him in God."

3: 3-4
But You, oh Lord, are a shield for Us.
Our glory and the lifter of Our heads.

We cried to the Lord with Our whole hearts,
and He heard Us out of His holy hill. Selah!

3: 5-8
We laid Us down and slept; We awaked:
For the Lord sustained Us (He was still with Me).

We will not be afraid of ten-thousands of people,
that have set themselves against Us roundabout.

Arise, and save Us, oh Our God:
For You have smashed all Our enemies on the cheek bone.
You have broken the teeth of the un-Godly.

Salvation belongs unto the Lord.
Your blessing (Fruits of the Spirit) is upon Your people.

4: 2
Oh, you sons of men (and the Devil and his bunch),
How long will you turn Our glory into shame?

How long will you love vanity and seek after vain intrigues?
Know that God has set apart him that is Godly for Himself.

5: 1-10
Give ear to Our words, oh Lord, and consider Our meditation,
and hearken to the voice of Our cry, Our King and Our God;
for unto thee will We pray. For in the morning will We pray unto thee.

Our voice will You hear in the morning, oh Lord,
In the morning will We direct Our prayer unto thee,
and will look up!

Lead Us oh Lord in Your righteousness, because of Our enemies.
Make Your way straight before Our face. For there
is no faithfulness in their mouth.

Their inward part is very wickedness. Their throat is an open sepulcher: they flatter with their tongue.

You, destroy them, oh God, Let them fall by their own counsels.
Cast them out in the multitude of their own transgression,
for they have rebelled against thee.

Part c

9: 15-20
The heathen is sunk down in the pit they made:
In the net which they hid is their foot taken.

The Lord is known by the judgment (His written word) which He executes.
The wicked are snared in the works of His own hands.

The wicked will be turned into hell, and all nations that forget God.

For the Needy (of Jesus - Christians) will not always be forgotten.
The expectation (Faith) of the Poor (in flesh – holy Christians) will not perish forever.

9: 15-20
Arise, oh Lord, let not man prevail. Let the heathen be judged in Your sight.
Put them in fear, oh Lord (of Hosts – angelic armies): that the
nations may know themselves to be but men.
Selah.

10: 1-3
Why do You stand so far off (Jesus)?
Why do You hide Yourself in times of trouble?

The wicked in his pride does persecute the Poor (Christian):
Let them be taken in the devices they have imagined.

10: 3-18
For the wicked boasts of his heart's desire, and blesses the covetous, whom
the Lord abhors. The wicked through the pride of his countenance
will not seek after God; God is not in all his thoughts.

His (Satan and his bunch) ways are always grievous. Your judgments are far above,
out his sight. As for all his enemies, he puffs at them. He has said in his heart,
"I will not be moved: for I will never be in adversity".

His (Satan) mouth is full of cursing and deceit and fraud:
and under his tongue is mischief and vanity.
He sits in the lurking places of the villages:

In secret places he does murder the Innocent.

His eyes are secretly set against the Poor (the Christian). He lies in wait secretly
like a lion in his den: He lies in wait to catch the Poor, and
he does catch the Poor, as he draws him into his net.

He crouches and humbles himself, that the Poor may fall by his strong ones.
He has said in his heart,

"God has forgotten; He hides His face: He will never see it."

Arise, oh Lord; Oh God, lift-up Your hand: forget not the humble.

Why does the wicked scorn God? He has said in his heart,
"God will not require it."

You have seen it; for You behold both mischief and spite, to requite (pay back) it with your hand.

Part d

10: 3-18

The Poor commits himself to You; You are a helper to the Fatherless (saints).

You break the arm of the wicked and evil man: Seek out his wickedness
until there be none. The Lord is king forever and ever:
The heathen is perished out of His land.

10: 3-18

Lord: You have heard the desire of the humble: You will prepare their
heart and cause Your ear to hear: To judge the Fatherless
and the oppressed, that the man of the earth (Satan)
oppresses no more.

11: 1-2

We put Our trust in the Lord:
How say you, "Flee as a bird to your mountain"?

You see the wicked bend their bow,
they make ready their arrow on the string,
that they may secretly shoot at the Upright in heart.

11: 3-7

If the foundations (faith - holiness – Ps. 119) be destroyed, what can the Righteous do?
The Lord is in His holy temple, His throne is in Heaven:
His eyes behold, His eyelids test, the children of men.

The Lord test the Righteous,
but the wicked and him that loves violence His soul hates.
On the wicked the Lord will rain down snares,
fire and brimstone, and a horrible tempest:
this will be the portion of their cup.

12: 1-8

Help, Lord, for the Godly man ceases, and the Faithful fail among the
children of men. They speak vanity everyone with his neighbor:
with flattering lips and double hearts do they speak.

The Lord will cut off all flattering lips, and the tongue that speaks proud things:
Who have said,
"With our tongues will we prevail. Our lips are our own,
who is Lord over us?"

For the oppression of the Poor, and for the sighing of the Needy, "Now will I arise,"
says the Lord, I will set him in safety from him (Satan) that puffs at him.

The words of the Lord are pure Words: as silver tried in the furnace of the earth, purified seven times. You will keep Us, oh Lord, You will preserve Us from this generation (the world system), forever.

The wicked walk on every side when vile men are exalted.

13:1-5
How long will You forget Us, oh Lord? Will You hide Your face from Us?
How long shall We take counsel in Our soul having sorrow in Our hearts daily?
How long shall Our enemies be exalted over Us.

Part e

13:1-5
Consider, and hear Us, oh Lord Our God:
Lighten Our eyes before We sleep the sleep of death.

Or Our enemy say,
"We have prevailed against Them":
And those that trouble Us rejoice when We are moved.

14: 4-5
Have all the workers of iniquity no knowledge.

Who eat up My people as they eat bread, who call not upon
the Lord: There (calling on His name) were they in fear:
for God is in the generation of the Righteous.

16: 5-11
The Lord is Our portion and the cup of Our inheritance.
You maintain Our lot (the Holy Ghost).

The lines (borders in Christ – Fruits of the Spirit) are fallen unto Us
in pleasant Places. Yes: We have a blissful heritage.

16: 7-9
We will bless the Lord, who has given Us counsel (His word). Our reins (the Will - integrity)
also instruct Us in the night season. We have set the Lord always before Us:
because He is at Our right hand, We shall not be moved.

*Therefore, Our hearts are glad and Our glory (soul) rejoices,
and Our flesh also rests in hope.*

17: 1-2, 7-13
Hear the right, oh Lord, and attend unto Our cry, and
give ear unto Our prayer that has no deceit in Our lips.

*Let Our sentence come forth from Your presence.
Let Your eyes behold the things that are equal.*

Show Your marvelous lovingkindness, oh You that saves by Your right hand (Holy Ghost)
Them which put Their trust in thee, from them that rise-up against Them.

Keep Us as the apple of Your eye under the shadow of Your wings.
From the wicked that oppress Us: from Our deadly
enemies that compass Us about.

They are enclosed in their own fat (self-will): with their mouth they speak proudly.

17: 1-2, 7-13

They (Satan and his bunch) have now surrounded Our steps: They have set their eyes
bowing down on the earth. Like a lion that is greedy of his prey,
and as it were a young lion lurking in secret places.

Arise oh Lord, disappoint him: cast him down:
Deliver Our soul from the wicked, which is Your sword:
from men which are Your right hand.

Part f

17: 1-2, 7-13
From men of this world which have their portion in this life: in whose belly
You fill with Your hidden treasure: they are full of children
and leave the rest of their substance to their babes.

We will behold Your face in righteousness:
We will be satisfied when We awake, with Your likeness.

18: 16-24, 32-50
He sent from above, He took and drew Us out of many waters.
He delivered Us from Our strong enemy, and from them
which hated Us: for they were too strong for Us.
They prevented Us in the day of Our calamity:
But the Lord was Our stay.

He has also brought Us forth out into a large Place (in Christ Jesus).
The Lord rewarded Us according to Our righteousness:
according to the cleanness of Our hands has He recompensed Us.
For You will save the afflicted people; but will bring down high looks.
For You will light Our candle: The Lord will enlighten our darkness.

18:29
For by thee can We run through a troop, and by Our God can We leaped over a wall.

As for God his way his way is perfect: The Word of the Lord is tested:
He is a buckler to Those that trust Him.

It is God that girds Us with strength and makes Our way perfect.
He makes Our feet like deer's feet and He sets Us upon the high Places (revelations of God).
He trains Our hands for war, so that a bow of steel is broken by Our arms.

You have also given Us the shield (Faith) of Your salvation:
and Your right hand has held Us up, and Your
gentleness has made Us great.

You have enlarged Our steps under Us to keep Our feet from sliding.
We have pursued Our enemies and overtaken them:
neither did We turn until they were consumed.

We have wounded them that they are not able to rise:
they are fallen under Our feet.

For You have girded Us with strength unto the Battle.
You have subdued under Us those that rose up against Us.

You have also given Us the necks of Our enemies,
that We might destroy them that hate Us.

18: 16-24, 32-50
Then did We beat them small as the dust before the wind:
We did cast them out as dirt in the streets.
You have delivered Us from the strivings of the people.

Part g

18: 16-24, 32-50
You have made Us (the Body of Christ) the head of the heathen.
A people that We have not known will serve Us.

It is God that avenges Us and subdues the people under Us. He delivers Us from Our enemies, yes, You
lift Us up from those that rise-up against Us: You have delivered Us from the violent man.

Therefore, We will give thanks unto thee, oh Lord, among the heathen and sing praises
unto Your name. You give great deliverances to Your kings (Believers - saints).

You show mercy to Your anointed, to David ((the Body of Christ - the Church), to his Seed (Me) forevermore.

21: 7-13
For We trust in the Lord, and through the mercy of the Most-High We shall not be moved.

Your hand will find out all Your enemies and Your right hand will find those
that hate You. You will make them as a fiery oven in the day of
Your anger. The Lord will swallow them up in His wrath,
and the fire will devour them.

You will destroy their offspring from the earth,
and their descendants from among the children of men.

For they intended evil against thee: they imagined a mischievous device
against thee, which they are not able to perform.

21: 12-13
You will make them turn their back when You make ready
Your arrows upon Your strings against the face of them.
Be thou exalted, oh Lord, in Your own strength,
and so will We sing and praise Your power.

22: 16-22
(Jesus ?)
For dogs (Spiritual wickedness) have surrounded Me roundabout.
The assembly of the wicked have enclosed Me: They have
pierced My hands and My feet. All My bones are
in place. They look and stare upon Me.

They part My garments among them and cast lots for My vesture. But be not
far off from Me, oh Lord, My strength, make haste to help Me.

Deliver My soul from the sword and My darling (soul) from the power of the Dog (Satan).
Save Me from the Lion's (Satan) mouth.

For You have heard Me from the horns of the unicorns.
I will declare Your name unto My brethren in the
middle of the Congregation will I praise You.

23:5
You prepare a table before Us in the presence of Our enemies:
You anoint Our heads with Oil; Our cup runs over.

Part h

25: 1, 15-22
Unto thee, oh Lord, do we lift-up Our souls. Oh Our God,
We trust in thee; let Us not be ashamed and
let not Our enemies' triumph over Us.
Our eyes are ever toward the Lord.
For He will pluck Our feet out of the net.

Consider Our enemies for they are many:
and they hate Us with a cruel hatred.

Lord, keep Our souls, and deliver Us:
Let Us not be put to shame, for We trust in You.

26: 1,19-11
Judge Us, oh Lord, for We have walked in Our integrity.

Gather not Our souls with sinners, nor Our lives with bloody men,
in whose hand is mischief and their right hand full of bribes.

27: 2-6, 11-14
When the wicked, even Our enemies and Our foes came upon Us
to eat up Our flesh, they stumbled and fell.

Though a host should encamp around Us, still We will not fear.
Though war should break out against Us, in this will We be confident.

One thing have We desired of the Lord that We will seek after: that We may
dwell in the House of the Lord all the days of Our lives: to behold
the beauty of the Lord and to inquire in His temple.
For in time of trouble He will hide
Us in His pavilion (in Christ).

Now shall Our heads be raised up above Our enemy round about Us.
Therefore, will We offer in His tabernacle sacrifices of joy.
We will sing, yes: We will sing praise to the Lord.

27: 11-14
Teach Us Your way, oh Lord, and lead Us in a plain path, because of Our enemies.

Deliver Us not over to the will of Our enemies,
for false witnesses have risen-up against Us,
and such as breathe out cruelty.

I had almost fainted unless I had believed to see the goodness of the Lord
in the land of the living. We will wait on the Lord and be of

good courage, and He will strengthen Our hearts:
We will wait on the Lord.

29: 11
The Lord will give strength to His people.
The Lord will bless His people with peace.

Part i

30: 1, 4, 14-18
We will extol thee, oh Lord; For You have lifted Us up,
and have not made Our foes to rejoice over Us.

Pull Us out of the net that they have secretly hid for Us: for You are Our strength.

30: 1, 4, 14-18
We trust (Believe) in You, oh Lord:
We said, "You are Our God: Our times are in Your hand".
Deliver Us from the hand of Our enemies, and from them that persecute Us.

Make Your face to shine upon Us: Save Us for Your mercy's sake.
Let Us not be ashamed, oh Lord: for We have called upon thee.
Let the wicked (unbelievers) be ashamed and let them be silent in the grave.

33: 17-19
A horse is a vain thing for safety: neither will he deliver any by his great strength.

*Behold the eye of the Lord is upon Them fear Him: upon Them that
hope in His mercy: to deliver Their soul from death and
to keep Them alive in time of famine.*

Our soul waits for the Lord: He only is Our help and Our shield.
For Our hearts will rejoice in Him, for We have trusted in His holy Name (Word).
Let Your mercy be upon Us, according as We have hoped in thee.

34: 14-17
Depart from evil and do good: seek peace and pursue it.
The eyes of the Lord are upon the Righteous,
and His ears are open to Their cry.

For the face of the Lord is against them that do evil,
To cut off the remembrance of them from the earth.

The Righteous cry and the Lord hears Them,
and delivers Them out of all Their troubles.

*The Lord is nigh unto all Them that are of a broken heart
and saves Them that be contrite of spirit.*

35: 1-8, 18-28
Plead Our cause, (Jesus), and fight against them that fight against Us.
Let them be confounded and ashamed that seek after Our soul.

Let them be turned back and brought to confusion that devise Our hurt.

Let them be as chaff before the wind: Let the angel of the Lord chase them away.

Let their way be dark and slippery, let the angel of the Lord persecute them.

35: 7-8, 18-26,
For without cause, have they hidden their net in a pit for Us.
Which, without cause, they have dug for Our soul.
Let destruction come upon them unawares,
and let the net that he has hid catch himself.

Part J

35: 7-8, 18-26,
We will give the thanks in the great Congregation:
We will praise You among the mighty (overcomers in Christ Jesus).

Let not them that are Our enemies wrongfully rejoice over Us:
Let them not wink with the eye that hate Us without cause.

For they speak not peace, but they devise deceitful matters
against Them that are quiet in the Land.

They open their mouth wide against Us,
saying,

"Aha, aha, our eyes have seen it."

This You have seen oh Lord: keep not silent: Oh Lord be not far
from Us. Stir up Yourself and awake to Our judgment,
even unto Our cause, Our God, and Our Lord.

Judge Us, oh Lord Our God, according to Your righteousness,
and let them not rejoice over Us. Let them not say in their hearts,
"Ah, so would we have it".
Let them not say,
"We have swallowed him up".

Let them be ashamed and confounded that rejoice over Our hurt.
Let them be clothed with shame and dishonor that
magnify themselves against Us.

36: 1-4, 11-12
Let not the foot of pride come against Us:
Let not the hand of the wicked remove.

There (God letting not) are the workers of iniquity fallen.
They are cast down and will not be able to rise.

37: 9-21, 28-40
For the evil doers will be cut off.
But They that wait on the Lord will inherit the earth.

For yet a little while, and the wicked will be no more. Yes, you will
consider diligently his place, but he will not be there.

But the Meek will inherit the earth and delight themselves in the abundance of peace.

35: 7-8, 18-26
The wicked plots against the Just, and gnashes upon Him with his teeth.
The Lord will laugh at him, for He sees that his day is coming.

The wicked have drawn out the sword and have bent his bow, to cast down
the Poor and Needy, to slay such as be Upright in conversation.

Their sword will enter their own heart, and their bows will be broken.

A little that the Righteous has is better than the riches of
many wicked. For the arms of the wicked are broken.

Part k

35: 24-26
The Lord upholds the Righteous. The Lord knows the days
of the Upright and their inheritance will be forever.

They will not be ashamed in the evil time (death) and in days of famine they will be satisfied.

But the wicked will perish, and the enemies of the Lord will be as the fat of lambs:
they will be consumed: into smoke will they be consumed away.

37:21, 28, 34-40
The wicked borrows without paying back.
But the Righteous shows mercy and gives:

For such as be blessed of the Lord will inherit the earth.
They that be cursed of Him will be cut off.

For the Lord loves judgment and forsakes not His saints.
They are preserved forever.

But the seed of the wicked will be cut off.

37:21, 28, 34-40
Our mouth brings forth Wisdom and Our tongue talks of judgment.
The law of Our God is in Our mouths and none of Our steps will slide.

The Lord will not leave Us in their hands, nor condemn Us when We are judged.

We will wait on the Lord and keep His way, and He will exalt Us to inherit the Land.
When the wicked are cut off We will see it.

I have seen the wicked in power, spreading himself like a
green bay tree. Yes, he passed away and was not.
Yes, I sought him, but he could not be found.

Mark the blameless man and behold the Upright,
for the end of that Man is peace.

But the transgressors will be destroyed together:
The end of the wicked will be cut off.

The salvation of the Righteous is of the Lord:
He is Our strength in time of trouble.

The Lord will help Us and deliver Us: He will deliver Us from the
wicked and save Us because We put Our trust (believe) in Him.

40: 13-17

Be pleased to deliver Us, oh Lord, and make haste to help Us.

Let them be ashamed and confounded together, that seek after

Our souls to destroy them.

Let them be driven backward and put to shame that wish Us evil.

40: 13-17

Let them be desolate for a reward of their shame,

that say, "Aha, aha."

But let all Those that seek thee rejoice and be glad in thee.

Let such as love Your salvation say continually,

"The Lord be magnified."

41: 4-7, 11-13

Lord be merciful unto Us and heal Our soul.

For We have sinned against thee.

Our enemies speak evil of Us. When will he die, and his name perish?

When he comes to see Me, he speaks vanity. His heart gathers iniquity

to itself. When he goes abroad, he tells it. All that hate Us

whisper together against Us, and devise Our hurt.

By this We know that You favor Us, because

Our enemies do not triumph over Us.

As for Us: You uphold Us in Our integrity,

and set Us before Your face forever.

Blessed be the Lord God of Israel from everlasting to everlasting.

(Blessed the be the Lord from "Once upon a time" to Kingdom come!)

Book 2

(15 minutes)

Part a

44: 4-8
You are Our King (Jesus), oh God: Command deliverances for Jacob (Zion – Body of Christ).

Through You We will push down Our enemies. Through Your name
will We tread under those that rise-up against Us.

For We will not trust in Our bow, neither will Our sword save Us.

You have saved Us from Our enemies and put them to shame that hated Us.
In God We boast all day long and praise Your name (Jesus) forever. Selah.

46: 1-5
God is Our refuge and strength, a very present help in trouble.
Therefore: We will not fear; Though the earth be removed,
and the mountains be carried in the midst of the sea.
Though the waters roar and be troubled.

Though the mountains shake with the swelling thereof.; Selah.

There is a River whose streams (Christians) make glad the City of God. Even
the holy dwelling Places of the Most High. God is in the midst of Her;
She shall not be moved. God will help Her, and that right early.

47: 1-9
Oh clap your hands all you people: shout unto God with a voice of triumph.
For the Lord Most High is terrible (in size): He is a great King over all the earth.
He will subdue the people under Us, and the nations under Our feet.

He will choose Our inheritance for Us, even the excellency of Jacob whom He loved. Selah.

God has gone up with a shout, the Lord with the sound of the trumpet.
Sing praises to God, sing praises: Sing praises unto Our King sing praises.
God reigns over the heathen: God sits upon the throne of His holiness.

The Princes of the peoples are gathered together, even the People of the God of Abraham:
for the Shields of the earth belong to God. He is greatly exalted.

48: 11-14
Let mount Zion (saved Jews) rejoice and let the Daughters of Judah be glad (Gentile Christians),
because of Your judgments (Your inheritance - sweeter than honey and better than money).
Walk about Zion: go around about Her:

Check out the towers thereof:
Mark well Her bulwarks:
and consider Her palaces
that We may tell it to the next generations.

For this God is Our God forever and ever: He will be Our guide
even unto death.

50: 3-5
Our God will come and not keep silent. A fire will devour before Him,
It will be very tempestuous round about Him. He will
call to the heavens above and to the earth,
that He may judge His people.

Gather My saints unto to Me, Those that have made a Covenant with Me by sacrifice (Fasting).

50: 16-22
The heavens will declare His righteousness, for God himself is judge. Selah.

But to the wicked God says,
"What have you to do to declare My statues,
or that you should take My covenant in your mouth?
Seeing you hate instruction and cast My words behind you.

When you saw a thief you consented with him, and have been partaker with adulterers.
You give your mouth to evil and your tongue frames deceit. You sit and
slander your brother: you slander your own mother's son.

These things you have done, and I kept silent.
You thought that I was altogether such a one as yourself:

But I will rebuke you to your face and set those things in order before your eyes.

Now consider this you that forget God, before I tear you in pieces
and there be none to deliver you."

52: 1-9
Why do you boast yourself in mischief oh mighty man? The goodness of God flows continually.
Your tongue devises mischiefs: like a sharp razor working deceitfully. You love evil
more than good, and lying rather than speaking righteousness. Selah.

You love all devouring words, oh you deceitful tongue.
God will destroy you forever, He will take you away, and pluck
you out of your dwelling place, and uproot you out of the land of the living.

The righteous shall also see and fear, and will laugh at him,
saying,

"Is this the man that made God not his strength.
But trusted in the abundance of his riches,
and strengthened himself in his wickedness.

But I AM: like a green olive tree in the House of God:
I will trust (Believe) in the mercy of God forever.

53:4-5
Have the workers of iniquity no knowledge?
That eat up My people like they eat bread?
They have not called upon God.

There (not calling on God), they (the wicked) were in great fear, where there was no fear.

For God has broken the bones of them that encamp against Us.
God has put them to shame because He has despised them.

Part c

54: 1-7

Save Us, oh God, by Your name (Word), and judge Us by Your strength.
Hear Our prayer, oh God; and give ear to the words of Our mouth.

For strangers are risen-up against Us and oppressors seek after Our souls.
They have not set God before them. Selah.

Behold God is Our helper; The Lord is with them that uphold Our souls.
God will reward evil to Our enemies; Cut them off in Your truth.
We will freely sacrifice unto You: We will praise Your name (Word),
oh Lord for it is good.

For He has delivered Us from all Our troubles
and Our eye has seen its desire upon Our enemies.

55: 6-11
I said,

"Oh that I had the wings of a dove! Then would I fly away and be at rest.
Behold, then would I wander off and remain in the Wilderness.
I would hasten my escape from the storm and tempest.

Destroy, oh Lord, and divide their tongues: For I have seen violence and strife
in the city. Day and night, they go about it upon the walls.
Mischief and sorrow are in the midst of it.

57: 3-4, 6
We will cry unto to God Most High and the Lord will send from Heaven
to save Us from the reproach of him that would swallow Us up.
God will send forth His mercy and Truth.

Our souls are among lions, even among them that are set on fire,
even the sons of men, whose teeth are spears and arrows,
and their tongue a sharp sword.

They have prepared a net for Our steps; Our souls are bowed down.
They have dug a pit before Us, into which they are fallen themselves.

58: 1-8, 10-11
Do you indeed speak righteousness, oh congregation?
Do you judge uprightly, oh you sons of men?

Yes, in heart you work wickedness, and you
weigh the violence of your hands in the earth.

The wicked are estranged from the womb: they go astray as soon as they be born, speaking lies. Their poison is like the poison of a serpent. They are like a deaf adder that stops her ear.

Which will not hearken to the voice of the charmers, charming never so wisely.

Break their teeth, oh God, in their mouth: break out the great teeth of the young lions (demons), oh God. Let them melt away as the waters that run continually.

Let them be cut in pieces when He bends His bow to shoot his arrows.

Part d

58: 10-11
As the snail melts, let everyone of them pass away. Like the untimely birth
of a woman, that they may not see the sun. Before Your pots (Christians)
can feel the thorns, He will take them away as with a whirlwind,
both living, and His wrath.

58: 1-8, 10-11
The righteous will rejoice when he sees this vengeance.
He will wash his feet in the blood of the wicked.
So that a man may say,

"Surely there is a reward for the Righteous.
Surely there is a God that judges in the earth."

59: 1-6, 9-11, 13-17
Deliver Us from Our enemies, oh Our God.
Defend Us from them that rise-up against Us.
Deliver Us from the workers of iniquity,
and save Us from bloody men.

For, lo, they lie in wait for Our souls.
The mighty are gathered against Us:
and not for Our transgression,
nor Our sin, oh Lord.

They run and prepare themselves without Our fault.
Awake to help Us and behold.

You, therefore, oh Lord God of Hosts (angel armies), the God of Israel,
Awake to visit all the heathen and
be not merciful to any wicked transgressors.

They return at evening and make a noise like a dog, and go around about the City.
Behold, they belch out with their mouth, swords are in their lips,
for who, say they, "Who does hear us?

But You oh Lord will laugh at them. You will have all the heathen
in derision. For the sin of their mouths and the words of
their lips. Let them be taken in their pride: and for
cursing and lying, which they speak.

Consume them in wrath, consume them: that they may not be:
and let them know that God rules in Jacob (the Body of Christ) unto the ends of the earth.

But We will sing of Your power, yes, We will sing of Your mercy in the morning:
For You have been Our defence and refuge in the day of Our trouble.

Unto thee, oh Our strength, will We sing: for God
is Our defence and the God of Our mercy.

62: 1-6
Truly Our souls wait upon God: from Him only comes Our salvation.
He only is Our rock and Our salvation:

He is Our defence, and We will not be greatly moved.

Part e

62: 1-6

How long will you imagine mischief against man?
All of you will be slain as a bowing wall
and as a tottering fence.

They only consult to take Him (the Christian) down from his excellency:
They delight in lies and they bless with their mouth:
but they curse inwardly.

Our souls will wait upon God, for Our expectation (Faith) is from Him.

He only is Our rock and Our salvation: He is Our defence,
and We will not be moved.

63: 8-10

Our souls follow hard after thee, oh Lord, Your right hand (Holy Ghost) upholds Us.

But those that seek after Our souls to destroy them,
will go down to the lowest parts of the earth.
They will fall by the Sword (the Word):
they will be a portion for foxes.

64: 1-10

Hear Our voice oh God, in Our prayer.
Preserve Our lives from fear of the enemy.
Hide Us from the secret council of the wicked,
and from the insurrection of the workers of iniquity.

They whet their tongue like a sword, and bend their bows
to shoot their arrows, even bitter words.

64: 4-9

That they may shoot in secret at the perfect:
Suddenly they shoot at him and fear not.

They encourage themselves in an evil matter:
they commune of laying snares privately.
They say, "Who will see us"?

They search out iniquities: They accomplish a diligent
search. Both the inward thought of every one
of them, and the heart is deep.

But God will shoot at them with an arrow. Suddenly will they be wounded.

They will make their own tongues to fall upon themselves.
All that see them will flee away.

The Lord said, "I will bring again from Bashan (Zion – the Body of Christ),
I will bring again My people from the depths of the sea (the world)."

That your foot may be dipped in the blood of your enemies,
and the tongue of your dogs in the same".

70: 1-5
Make haste, oh God, to deliver Us: Make haste to help Us, oh Lord.
Let them be ashamed and confounded that seek after Our souls:
Let them be turned backward and brought to confusion,
that devise Our hurt.

Let them be turned back for a reward of their shame,
that say, "Aha, aha."

But let all Those that seek thee rejoice and be glad in thee.
and let such as love Your salvation, say continually,
"Let the Lord be magnified."

We are Poor (of this world and flesh) and Needy (of Jesus): Make haste unto Us, oh God;
You are Our help and deliverer, oh Lord: make no tarrying!

71: 1-3
In thee, oh Lord, do We put Our trust, let Us never be put to shame.
Deliver Us in Your righteousness and cause Us to escape.
You be Our strong habitation whereunto We may continually resort.

Book 3

Part a

73: 1-12
Truly God is good to Israel, even to Such as be of a clean heart (blood – Fasting).

My feet were almost gone; My steps had nearly slipped.

For I was envious of the foolish (un-Godly), when I saw the prosperity of the wicked.
For there are no bands in their death, but their strength is firm.

They are not in trouble as other men, neither are they plagued like
other men. Therefore, pride compasses them as a chain,
and violence covers them as a garment.

Their eyes stand out with fatness,
and they have more than their heart could wish for.
They are corrupt and speak wickedly concerning oppression:
they speak loftily.

They set their mouths against the heavens, and their tongues walks
through the earth. Therefore, his people return here,
and waters of a full cup are wrung out to them.

They say, "How does God know? Is there knowledge in the most High?

Behold, these are the un-Godly that prosper in the world,
they increase in riches.

Surely You have set them in slippery places.
You cast them down into destruction.

How are they brought in desolation as in a moment!
They are utterly consumed with terrors.

But it is good for Us to draw near to God: We have put Our trust (believing) in God:
We have put Our trust in the Lord God, that We may declare all Your works.

74: 10-22
Oh God, how long shall the enemy reproach? Shall the enemy blaspheme forever?

Why do You withdraw Your hand, even Your right hand? Pluck it out of Your bosom.

For God is Our King of old working salvation in the midst of the earth.

You divided the sea by Your strength, You break the heads of the
dragons in the waters. You break the heads of Leviathan

in pieces, and gave him to be meat for Them
inhabiting the Wilderness (in Christ).

74: 15-19

You did stop the fountain and the flood: You dried up mighty rivers. The day is Yours,
the night is also Yours: You prepared the light and the sun. You set all the
borders of the earth: You made summer and winter.

Part b

74: 15-19
Remember this that the enemy has reproached oh Lord,
and the foolish people have blasphemed Your name.

Oh, deliver not the soul of Your turtle dove
unto the multitude to the wicked.

74: 19-23
Have respect unto the Covenant (the Word of His power)
for the dark places of the earth are full of the habitations of cruelty.

Arise, oh Lord and plead Your own cause: Remember
how the foolish man reproaches You daily.

Forget not the voice of Your enemies, the tumult of
those that rise-up against thee increases daily.

75: 10
The Lord God will cut off the horn of the wicked.
But the horn of the Righteous will be exalted.

76: 1-12
In Judah is God known; His name is great in Israel.
His tabernacle is in (Jeru) Salem and His dwelling place in Zion.
There (in Zion – the Body of Christ) broke He the arrows of the bow, the shield,
the sword, and the battle. Selah.

You are more glorious and excellent than the mountains of prey.

The stouthearted are spoiled, they have slept their sleep,
and none of the men of might have found their hands.
At Your rebuke, oh God, both the chariot
and the horse are cast into a deep sleep.

You, even You, are to be feared.
Who can stand in Your sight once You become angry?

You did cause judgment to be heard from heaven.
The earth feared and was still. When God rose to judgment;
to save the Meek (holy Ones of Israel – holy Christians) of the earth.

Instead of smoldering rage – God praise. All that sputtering rage now a garland for God.

He will cut off the spirit of princes. He is terrible to the kings of the earth.

77: 16-19

The waters (the seas of peoples and thoughts) saw thee, oh God, the waters saw thee,
oh God, and were afraid.
The depths also were troubled: the clouds poured out water:
the skies sent out a sound: Your arrows also went abroad.

The voice of Your thunder (His word) was heard in the heavens. The lightnings
lightened the world: the earth trembled and shook at Your way in the sea:
Your paths are in the great waters (the seas of peoples and thoughts):
and Your footsteps are not known.

Book 4

(10 minutes)

Part a

92: 8-11
But You oh Lord, are Most High forevermore.
For lo: Your enemies, oh Lord: Your enemies shall perish:
all the workers of iniquity shall be scattered.

But Our horn (Fruits of the Spirit) will You exalt like the horn of a Unicorn.
We are anointed with fresh Oil (the Holy Ghost).

Our eyes will also see Our desire upon Our enemies.
Our ears will hear Our desire of the wicked that rise-up against Us.

94: 1-6
OH LORD GOD to whom vengeance belong: OH GOD to whom vengeance belong:
Show Yourself, and lift-up Yourself,
you judge of the earth: render a reward to the proud.

94: 4-6
Lord, how long shall the wicked? How long shall the wicked triumph?
How long will they utter and speak hard things? and all
the workers of iniquity boast themselves?

They break in pieces Your people, oh Lord, and afflict Your heritage (Body of Christ).

They slay the Widow and the Stranger and murder the Fatherless.

Blessed is the man You chasten, oh Lord: and teach Them out of Your law.

That You may give Him rest from the days of adversity till the pit be dug for the wicked.

For the Lord will not cast off His people: neither will He forsake His inheritance.
But judgment will return to Righteousness, and all the Upright in heart will follow it.

Who will rise-up for Me against the evil doers?
Who will stand up for Me against the workers of iniquity?
(I will)

We would of dwelt in silence unless the Lord had been Our help.

97: 9-11
For You, oh Lord are high above all the earth: You are exalted above all gods.
You that love the Lord hate evil: He preserves the souls of His saints:
He delivers them out of the hand of the wicked!

Light is sown for the Righteous, and gladness for the Upright in heart.

101:8
The Lord will early destroy all the wicked of the land.
That He may cut off all the wicked doers from the City of the Lord.

104: 14-15
The Lord would not let no man do Them wrong. Yes, He reproved kings for
Their sakes. saying, "Touch not My anointed and do My prophets no harm".

Book 5

(15 minutes)

Part a

107: 1-2 8, 21-22
Then they cried to the Lord and He delivered them in their distress, and
He led Them forth by the right Way, that They might go to a
City of Habitation (Zion – the Body of Christ - Heaven).

For He has broken the gates of brass and cut in half the bars of iron.

We cried unto the Lord in Our trouble and the Lord heard Us, and delivered
Us out of all Our distresses. He sent out His word and healed Us
and delivered Us from all Our troubles.

He makes the storm a calm, so that the waves are stilled.
He turns rivers into a wilderness and water springs into dry ground.

108: 13
Through God We shall do valiantly: For it is He, that treads down Our enemies.

109: 7-14, 19-20, 28-29
Let the wicked be judged and condemned: and let his prayer become sin.
Let his days be few and let another take his office.
Let his children be fatherless and his wife a widow.

Let the extortioner catch all that he has.
Let strangers spoil all his labor.
Let there be none to extend mercy to him.
Let there be none to favor his fatherless children.

Let his posterity be cut off.
Let their name be blotted out of the following generation.
Let the iniquity of their fathers be remembered with the Lord.
Let not the sin of his mother be blotted out.

Let them be before the Lord continually, that He may cut off the memory
of them from the earth. Because that he remembered not to
show mercy, but persecuted the Poor and Needy man
that he might even slay the broken of heart.

As he loved cursing so let it come unto him. As he delighted not in blessing,
so let it be far from him. As he clothed himself with cursing as
with a garment, so, let it come into his bowels
like water, and into his bones like oil.

Let it be unto him as a garment that covers him, and for a girdle wherewith
he is girdled continually. Let this be the reward of Our adversaries
from the Lord, and of them that speak evil against Our souls.

109: 7-4, 9-20, 28-29
Let them curse, but You bless Us Lord. When they arise let them be ashamed,
but let Your servants rejoice. Let Our adversaries be clothed
with shame, and let them cover themselves with their
own confusion, as with a mantle

Part b

114: 1-8
When Israel went out of Egypt, the House of Jacob
from a people of a strange language.

Judah was His Sanctuary and Israel His dominion.

The sea saw it and fled: Jordan was driven back. The mountains
skipped like rams and the little hills like lambs.

What ails you, oh sea that you have fled: and you Jordan that you were driven back?
You mountains, that you skipped like rams and you little hills like lambs?

Tremble you earth at the presence of the Lord. at the presence of the God of Jacob (the Church),
Who turned the rock into standing water, and the flint into a fountain of waters.

118: 7-12
The Lord has taken Our part with them that help Us:
Therefore, We shall see Our desires upon them that hate Us.
It is better to trust in the Lord than to put your confidence in man.
It is better to trust (Believe) in the Lord than to put your confidence in princes.

All nations compassed Us about, but in the Name of the Lord, We will destroy them.
They compassed Us about, yes, they compassed Us about, but in the
Name of the Lord (of Jesus), We will destroy them

They compassed Us about like bees.
They are quenched as the fire of thorns,
for in the Name of the Lord We will destroy them.

For the wicked has thrust sore through Us that We might fall,
but the Lord helps Us.

Ps. 119
You have rebuked the proud that are cursed,
which do err from Your commandments.

23
Princes also sit and speak against Us,
but We meditate on Your statues.

42
So shall We have an Answer for him who reproaches Us,
for We trust in Your word.

51

The proud have had Us in great derision,

but We have not declined from Your law (Law of the House - holiness).

69

The proud have forged a lie against Us,

but We will keep Your precepts with Our whole heart.

78

Let the proud be ashamed for they have dealt perversely (crookedly) with Us,

without a cause, but We will meditate in Your precepts.

Part c

95

The wicked have waited to destroy Us:
but We will consider Your testimonies.

110

They have laid a snare for Us:
but We erred not from Your precepts.

119

You put away all the wicked of the earth like dross (garbage):
and that is why We love Your testimonies (word).

134

Deliver Us from the oppression of man:
and so, will We keep Your precepts.

161

Princes have persecuted Us without a cause:
but Our heart stands in awe of Your word.

50

This is Our comfort in affliction; Your word has quickened Us!

125: 1- 4

They that trust in Lord shall be as Mount Zion which cannot be removed,
but abides forever.

As the mountains are roundabout Jerusalem,
so is the Lord roundabout His people,
from this time forth and forevermore.

127: 3-5

Lo, children are a heritage (property) of the Lord and the fruit of the womb is His reward.
As arrows are in the hand of a warrior, so are children of the youth.
Happy is the man that has his quiver full of them:

They shall not be ashamed, but they shall speak with the enemies in the gate.

129: 4-5

The Lord is righteous:
He has cut in half the cords of the wicked.
Let them all be confounded and turned back that hate (forget) Zion.
Let them be as the grass upon the housetops that withers before it grows.

137: 8-9

Oh Daughter of Babylon (the world system) who is to be destroyed.
Happy shall he be that rewards you as you have served Us.

Happy shall he be that takes and dashes your little ones against the stones.

138: 6-8

Though the Lord be high, yet He has respect unto the Lowly.
But the proud He knows a far off.
Though We walk in the midst of trouble You will quicken Us.

You will stretch forth Your hand against the wrath of Our enemies,
and Your right hand will save Us.

Part d

140: 1-13

Deliver Us from the evil man: preserve Us from the violent man.
Who imagine mischiefs in the heart.

They are continually gathered against Us for war. They have sharpened their
tongues like a serpent: snake poison is under their lips. Selah.

Keep Us, oh Lord from the hands of the wicked. Preserve Us from the
violent man who has purposed to overthrow Our goings.

The proud have hid a snare for Us, and cords.
They have spread a net by the wayside.
They have set gins for Us. Selah.

We said to the Lord, "You are Our God": hear the voice of Our supplications,
oh Lord. Oh God the Lord, the strength of Our salvation.

You have covered Our heads in the day of battle.
Grant not, oh Lord the desires of the wicked,
or they will exalt themselves. Selah.

As for the heads of those that compass Us about,
let the mischief of their own lips cover them.

Let burning coals fall upon them: Let them be cast into the
fire and deep pits, that they rise not up again.

Let not an evil speaker be established in the earth:
Evil will hunt down the violent man to overthrow him.

I know that the Lord will maintain the cause of the Afflicted (Christians in their testing's)
and the right of the Poor. Surely the Righteous will give thanks to
Your name (Jesus): the Upright will dwell in Your presence.

141; 1-4, 9-10

Lord We cry to You; make haste to Us.
Give ear to Our voice when We cry to You.
Let Our prayer be set before You as incense,
and the lifting-up of Our hands as the evening sacrifice.

Set a watch oh Lord over Our mouths; keep the door Our lips. Incline not Our hearts
to any evil thing, to practise wicked works with men that work iniquity:
Let Us not eat of their dainties.

213

142: 5-7
We cried to You, oh Lord: We said,
"You are Our refuge and Our portion in the land of the living".
Attend unto Our cry for We are brought very low.

Deliver Us from Our persecutors; for they are stronger than Us.

Bring Our soul out of prison, that We may praise Your name.
The Righteous will compass Us about. You
will deal bountifully with Us.

Part e

143: 1-12

Hear Our prayer oh Lord, and give ear to Our supplications:
Answer Us in Your faithfulness, and righteousness.
Enter not into judgment with Us, for in Your sight
no living man will be justified.

For the enemy has persecuted Our souls.
He has smitten Our lives down to the ground:
He has made Us to dwell in darkness,
as those that be a long time dead.

Therefore, Our spirits are overwhelmed within Us;
Our heart within Us are desolate.
But We remember the Days of old.

We meditate on all Your works.
We muse on the works of Your hands.
We stretch forth Our hands to You:
Our soul's thirst for You as in a dry and thirsty land.
Selah.

Hear Us speedily, oh Lord: Our spirits fail.
Hide not Your face from Us, before We be
like those that go down into the pit.

Cause Us to hear Your lovingkindness in the morning.
For in You do We trust; cause Us to know the way
wherein we should walk; for We lift-up Our souls to You.
Deliver Us from Our enemies, for We lift-up Our souls unto You.

143: 1-12

Deliver Us, oh Lord, from Our enemies: For We flee to You to hide Us.

Teach Us to do Your will; for You are Our God:
Lead Us into the land (the Word) of uprightness.

Quicken Us, oh Lord, for Your name's sake. For Your righteousness' sake
bring Our souls out of trouble, and of Your mercy cut off
Our enemies, and afflict all them that afflict Our souls,
for We are Your servants.

144: 5-8, 11

Bow down Your heavens, oh Lord, and come down:
Touch the mountains and they will smoke.

Cast forth Your lightning and scatter them.
Shoot out Your arrows and destroy them.

Send Your hand from above. Rid Us and deliver Us out
of great waters, from the hand of strange children.

Whose mouth speaks vanity, and their right hand
is a right hand of falsehood.

144: 5-8, 11
That Our sons may be as plants grown up in their youth.
That Our daughters may be as corner stones,
polished in the likeness of a palace.

That Our storehouses may be full of all kinds of store,
that Our sheep may bring forth thousands,
and ten thousand in Our streets.

That Our oxen may be strong to labour.
That there be no breaking in or going out.
That there be no complaining in Our streets.

Happy is the people that be in such a case:
Yes, happy is the people whose God is the Lord.

147: 5-7
Great is the Lord, and of great power; His understanding is infinite.
The Lord lifts-up the Meek holy (Christians),
but casts the wicked down to the ground.

P.S

Isa. 59
As for Me (God), this is My covenant (Contract) with Them, says the Lord,
My Spirit which is upon You, and My words which I have put in Your mouth,
will not depart out of Your mouth, nor out of the mouth of Your seed,
nor out of the mouth of Your seed 'seed, says the Lord,
from now on, and forevermore.

Duet. 6
These Words that I command You this day will be in Your heart.
You will teach them diligently to Your children, and
will talk of them when You sit in Your house,
and when You walk in the way,
when You lie down, and
when You rise-up.

Ps. 132
"If Your children will keep My covenant and My testimony that I will teach Them,
then Their children will also sit upon Your throne!

Who champion My will cause against the wicked?
Who will stand up for Me against the evil doers?

I will.

————————————————